1 INTRODUCTION

Since becoming involved in treasure hunting some 40 years ago, the burning question for me has always been: How can I find more treasure in less time? Not that I am impatient or don't find pleasure in the pursuit itself; it is just that finding more, faster, is surely the route to success. I read the books and the magazines and there is plenty of good advice. Buy the best equipment you can afford. Develop your skills. Research thoroughly. Good advice but is it enough? The majority of treasure locations are unknown and most finds are accidental. Or are they?

Reading through the treasure hunting magazines there are countless stories of finds being made in remarkable circumstances. Many treasure hunters make good finds 'after only five minutes searching' or 'walking back to the car' or 'having dreamt of treasure' and so on. I may have believed this to be exaggeration, if I hadn't started having similar experiences – the usual format being a casual discussion about a particular object followed by recovering a similar object almost immediately. Some put this phenomenon down to luck or coincidence, while others give it fancy names such as Serendipity, Assonance or the X-Factor. It happened so many times to me that I knew there must be more to it. What was the nature of this phenomenon and could it be harnessed? I tried deliberately saying 'I am going to find (a certain object)' before searching and even chanting 'I want gold' during a search. But it never did any good. Then I heard about dowsing.

When I looked into dowsing it wasn't just about specially gifted people

DOWSING FOR TREASURE
The New Successful Treasure Hunter's
Essential Dowsing Manual

David Villanueva

Copyright © 2016 David Villanueva

All rights reserved. Nothing may be reproduced from this work or stored in any form of information retrieval system without the express written permission of the publisher.

The author and publisher issue this manual on the understanding that while every effort has been made to ensure the accuracy of all the information presented, no liability will be accepted for any loss or profit, direct or otherwise as a consequence of using any of the information presented. The opinions given are those of the author who is acting in good faith according to extensive research undertaken by him and who confirms that he himself uses the principles described

**ISBN-10: 1518766064
ISBN-13: 978-1518766060**

DEDICATION

To James (Jimmy) Longton, (1930 - 2015) a true friend.

CONTENTS

	Acknowledgments	i
1	INTRODUCTION	1
2	A BRIEF HISTORY OF DOWSING	4
3	HOW DOES DOWSING WORK?	8
4	WHY NOT JUST USE A METAL DETECTOR?	11
5	FINDING AND USING A DOWSER	13
6	THE PENDULUM	15
7	MAP DOWSING	21
8	THE L-ROD	25
9	TO BAIT OR NOT TO BAIT	39
10	BUILDING A BETTER GOLD TRAP	43
11	TO LOOK FOR OR TO UNLOOK FOR	45
12	BUYING A BETTER GOLD TRAP	47
13	ALL THAT GLITTERS	50
14	METAL DETECTORS AND SEARCH HEADS	55
15	PHOTOGRAPHING TREASURE AURAS	62
16	RESEARCH	66
17	PUTTING IT ALL TOGETHER	71
18	TREASURE HUNTING BASICS	80
19	SEARCH AGREEMENTS	89
20	BIBLIOGRAPHY	91
21	BOOKS IN PRINT FROM THE SAME AUTHOR	93

ACKNOWLEDGMENTS

While, for obvious reasons, there is much secrecy in treasure hunting, now and again you come across kind gentlemen who willingly share their knowledge, expertise and even their equipment! I owe a debt of gratitude to: Jimmy Longton, Kybob, Glenn, Takis, Mike Scott, Frank Delamere Richard and David. Thank you gentlemen.

finding water, as I thought, almost anybody could find absolutely anything large or small. The best treasure dowsers could locate treasure, hundreds or thousands of miles away using a simple tool with a map, then go out into the field and dig it up. Although dowsing still hasn't been scientifically proven it was certainly worth investigating as the possible answer to a treasure hunter's prayers.

I read books on dowsing, most were obsessive about finding water, some were academic, and there were one or two practical guides on the techniques of dowsing but almost nothing on treasure dowsing. I bought a pair of L shaped rods and tried to follow the instructions with little effect. I didn't know what the problem was at the time and assumed I was one of the very few people unable to dowse. Looking back, the problem was the instructor had devised the most impractical way imaginable to use a pair of L-rods.

I all but forgot about dowsing until I heard about Jimmy Longton. Jimmy was offering to dowse maps for a small fee or percentage of the finds. More as an experiment than anything, I sent Jimmy a map of a field, which had already yielded a little treasure. A couple of days later Jimmy phoned me rather excitedly about the potential of the site: "There's gold and silver everywhere." He said. When the map arrived back, it was littered with crosses; some indicated iron but most indicated non-ferrous metal. Immediately, I noticed that most of the crosses were concentrated in the area where I had already made finds and a row of ferrous crosses coincided with a row of iron stakes on the site. Jimmy lived 300 miles away and had never visited the site, I hadn't told him anything about the site either, so how did he know? Using Jimmy's map I went on to double the amount of finds I recovered from the site.

More importantly, as well as the map, Jimmy had sent me instructions on how to make and use L-rods for treasure dowsing. Jimmy's instructions were clearly practical from someone who knew what he was talking about. I followed his instructions and quickly learned to dowse. I confess to being a poor dowser compared to Jimmy. Even so my treasure hunting success rate has improved remarkably to the extent that I have not only held one or more metal detecting club annual trophies for a number of years but I have all but lost count of the number of treasure finds I have had to report since the introduction of the UK Treasure Act in 1997.

Through this manual, I am aiming to draw on my own and others' experience in the practical use of dowsing to aid the location of treasure. You do not necessarily need to become a dowser yourself, you can easily find a dowser to do the job for you or use this manual to teach a friend or relative. This is a practical guide to the best ideas for supercharging your treasure hunting; use the ideas and I guarantee you will be amazed at the results. **Good Hunting!**

2 A BRIEF HISTORY OF DOWSING

Dowsing has been recorded since the time of Moses, for the story of Aaron producing water from the rock (Exodus chapter 17, verse 6) is often quoted as the first written evidence. Even if we dismiss the Biblical claim, dowsers appear engraved on ancient Egyptian stonework and on the statue of a Chinese emperor dating circa 2200BC. Little else of dowsing is recorded until Agricola wrote *De Re Metallica*, in 1556, a composition on mining, which included an illustration of German dowsers at work.

Illustration from *De Re Metallica*

Almost a hundred years after Agricola, Martine de Bertereau, Baroness de Beausoleil travelled Europe, with her husband, locating mineral deposits by dowsing. They discovered over 150 ore deposits of iron, gold and silver in France alone, before being imprisoned for practicing the 'black arts'. Later, in the same century, a particularly interesting book was written by Jean Nicholas de Grenoble published in Lyons in 1691 under the title of **La Verge de Jacob or L'arte de Trouver les Trésors: Les Sources, les Limites, les Métaux, les Mines, les Minéraux et autres choses cachés par L'usage du Baton fourché.** *(The Rod of Jacob or the art of finding treasure, springs, boundaries, metals, mines, minerals and other hidden things, by the use of the forked twig)*. Dowsing then seems to have sunk back into obscurity, although, undoubtedly it continued to be practiced, at least for finding of water — the lifeblood of all living things — practiced in secrecy, perhaps, because of its occult associations and the Church's condemnation as the work of the devil.

Victorian scientific interest aided by a softening of the Church's attitude brought dowsing out into the open. In 1874, Thomas Welton translated and published Jean Nicholas' book in English. During the following decades a number of respected men, including the physicist, Albert Einstein, performed impressive feats with a variety of dowsing devices. Most of these feats were only of academic value but by the middle of the 20th century dowsing was regularly being put to a great variety of profitable uses.

Colonel Harry Grattan, CBE, Royal Engineers was given the task of building a new Headquarters for the British Rhine Army at Mönchen Gladbach, Germany in 1952. Planning for at least 9000 people who would need 750,000 gallons of water per day was a major project. Water supply was a big problem. Notwithstanding that the British Army preferred the security of its own water supply, the three local waterworks would have had to upgrade their equipment and pass the high costs on in the form of water rates at £20,000 ($30,000) per year — a huge sum then.

Colonel Grattan knew of a nearby family with a private well, which produced better quality water than any of the waterworks. He employed a geologist with the intention of tapping this source but a trial bore produced very little water. The Colonel was a proficient dowser and decided to use his skills to solve the problem. Using the traditional forked twig the colonel began dowsing and getting reactions everywhere to the west of the test bore. On the strength of this, two further trial bores were executed with spectacular results.

The trials showed that the ground was mainly solid clay, but between 73 and 96 feet down there was an aquifer, which produced a copious supply of excellent quality water. The German government, responsible for site construction, was less than convinced by such surveying techniques and were adamant that the water supply would soon dry up. Gaining the support of his superior, General Sugden, Colonel Grattan was able to continue his exploration. Dowsing from horseback, the colonel plotted out the full extent of the aquifer, which extended to within a few hundred yards of two of the waterworks. The British Rhine Army's private waterworks were constructed providing the Army with all the water it needed and savings running into millions of pounds over the years.

Somewhat closer to our quest for buried treasures was the work of Major General Scott Elliot, a former president of the British Society of Dowsers who spent many years finding previously unknown archaeological sites by dowsing. His initial plan was that he would find the sites and then hand them over for professional excavation. On discovering that the professionals were not interested, partly through skepticism and partly because they had more than enough sites of their own, the major learned to do his own excavations. He also discovered he could save enormous amounts of time and effort by mapping out the site features by dowsing before he removed the first sod. Nothing spectacular in terms of finds of great intrinsic value were ever reported but nevertheless, over a period of some 20 years the major discovered and excavated an impressive list of sites.

The fairly recent development of treasure hunting as a popular hobby has drawn one or two dowsers to the challenge of using their skills to find buried metal artifacts. In the USA, the late Louis J Matacia was a surveyor who studied dowsing for years. During the Vietnam War he was commissioned to teach dowsing skills to US Marines so that they could avoid booby traps, navigate safely through jungles and learn the whereabouts of the enemy. Soldiers reported that using the L-rod in this way saved many lives. Louis was particularly interested in the challenge of the search. Using his dowsing together with a range of scientific devices he located lost pipes, oil, wells, caves and buried treasures.

The most successful treasure dowser in Britain was the late Jimmy Longton from Lancashire. Jimmy took up dowsing after retiring from boxing to first hit the headlines for his part in the finding of the Viking (c. 930 AD) silver brooch hoard (cache) near Penrith, Cumbria. The two largest (i.e. longest) thistle brooches were found previously in 1785 and 1830 (largest) in a field called silver field. Jimmy and his friend Gerald Carter located and investigated the field in 1989 and recovered five more brooches, which were subsequently declared Treasure Trove. The award was more than £40,000 GB Pounds ($60,000). His most recent find is potentially Britain's Tutankhamen: a seventeenth century shipwreck, believed to contain untold treasures, including a 230 piece gilt-silver dinner service once owned by Charles I.

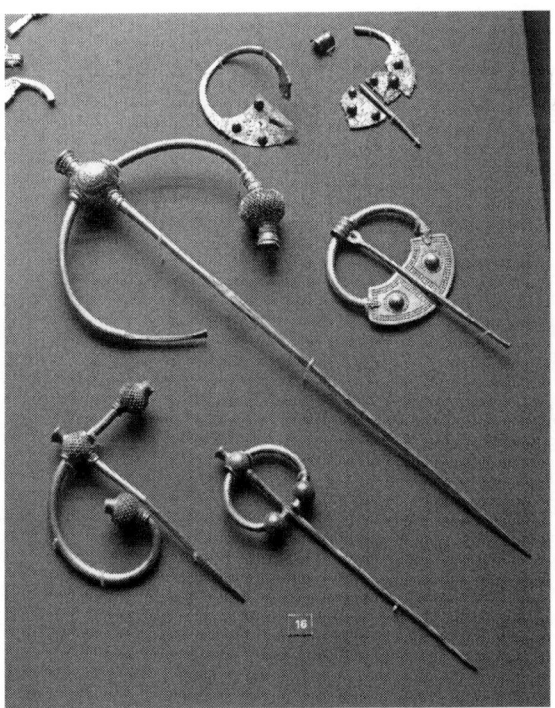

The Penrith Hoard in the British Museum Copyright 2010 Ealdgyth and reused under a Creative Commons Attribution-Share Alike 3.0 Unported license

3 HOW DOES DOWSING WORK?

No one knows how dowsing works for sure, they only know that it does. There are two popular theories to explain dowsing: the first suggests that dowsing works as a result of natural phenomena. Buried metal, minerals and underground water causes either a magnetic field or a disturbance in the Earth's own magnetic field. It is thought the dowsing rod is an amplifying tool for showing the reaction of the magnetic field in the ground to the natural magnetic field of the body.

This theory was investigated scientifically in Logan, Utah, USA, over 30 years ago. Intrigued by a dowser pinpointing the bodies of two boys who sadly drowned in a local river, Duane G. Chadwick, professor at the Utah State University Water Research Laboratory undertook several experiments to see if there was some scientific basis for dowsing. Chadwick and his colleague, Larry Jensen started from the known observations of geologists that underground water can cause anomalies in the Earth's magnetic field. They figured that dowsers could show sensitivity to these anomalies by involuntary muscular movement in the wrists and dowsing rods would certainly amplify any small muscular reaction by up to 300 times.

In the first of a series of experiments, on the Campus, they set about testing the idea that dowsing reactions might coincide with the spots where some changes occurred in the Earth's magnetic field. Chadwick and Jensen laid out a straight track, free of obstructions and, using a cesium vapor magnetometer, checked for variations in the Earth's magnetic field at one-foot intervals. Chadwick then buried a length of wire, in a neutral area, to distort the magnetic field. Twenty-five people were recruited to walk the test course. Few of them were dowsers; most were students or university staff. They were given a pair of L-shaped rods made out of clothes-hanger wire, and told to hold them out roughly horizontal. If they felt any kind of reaction, they were to stop and put down a small block of wood. The results were amazing in that 23 of the participants had a dowsing reaction within three feet of the buried wire. As Chadwick remarked: "With odds like that you could break the bank."

In another experiment in North Logan City Park, Chadwick and Jensen marked out a test course with no obvious or known features. This time, the test was double blind - nothing was deliberately buried and no one knew what was out there. 150 participants with dowsing rods were asked to drop a wooden block whenever they experienced a dowsing reaction and again almost everyone did. They dropped an average of 11.3 blocks each and the location of each block was documented. Then Chadwick and Jensen went over the course with two magnetometers mounted, at different heights, on a wooden sled. The difference between the magnetometer readings showed the variation in the magnetic field along the track walked by the dowsers. The researchers then graphed the magnetometer readings against the positions of the wooden blocks, which showed again that the dowsing reactions occurred unmistakably at peaks in the magnetic field.

It may not be just magnetism itself. Pierre Beasse in: **A New and Rational Treatise of Dowsing...**, first published in 1941 as an English translation of the 1938 second French edition, explains how:

Under the action of the *electric field* of the Earth, any body emits:

1. On *all surfaces* and both in the direction of the zenith [top] and in the opposite direction, *a thick bundle of vertical rays*.

2. On a *special line* of that [top] surface, two *thin sheets* of rays with the respective inclination of 45 degrees and 135 degrees on the vertical.

Some cameras can capture the radiation produced by buried metal.

Radiation emanating from a buried iron pipe

It is reasonable to assume that the human body can tune into this radiation and react to it. The dowsing rod may just act as an amplifier to human reactions of which we are not normally aware. Or is there more to it?

Another theory is that dowsing works through the paranormal; an explanation accounting for the ability of some dowsers to find things thought not to produce or influence magnetic fields. As far as field dowsing (i.e. dowsing in close proximity to the object or substance being sought) is concerned, the paranormal theory is probably in error since virtually everything animal, vegetable or mineral, reacts to magnetic fields.

Map dowsing is something else. How does a person dowse a map to successfully locate a 'target' (as dowsers tend to call objects they are trying to find) hundreds or thousands of miles away? Are we able to pick up radiation from buried objects at great distances as a radio receiver picks up radio waves? There are many unanswered questions, which are commonly put down to psychic ability or intuition. Mankind does not know everything. Much science today was science fiction and mysticism of the past and dowsing has undoubtedly survived from primitive times when the ability to find water may have meant the difference between life and death.

There seems to be two types of dowsing: field dowsing based on magnetic effects and map dowsing or distance dowsing probably based on intuition or psychic ability. The two types of dowsing are quite different and both types can be learned and improved with perseverance and practice. Either type, used alone can bring impressive results; put the two together and the results can be spectacular.

4 WHY NOT JUST USE A METAL DETECTOR?

Metal detecting is easy – you only need to put the search head in the right place to make great treasure finds. The less easy part is deciding where to put the search head! Research will help the decision but even then you will probably be detecting a large area of land with a small search head.

Let's look at search methods. We will assume you have a site to search, 69 yards (or meters) wide by 70 yards (or meters) long. That's roughly one acre or a little less than half a hectare. Buried in the site are five treasures within detection range, each marked with a cross.

You could do a systematic search with a metal detector, covering every square inch. If your overlapping search sweep averages 1.5 yards (or meters) you would need to cross the site 46 times and walk nearly two miles or three kilometers. It would take a few hours, but you should get 100% of the treasure finds.

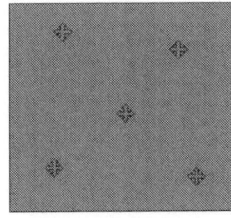

Systematic Search: 100% of the time for 100% of the treasure

Some treasure hunters or metal detectorists search randomly.

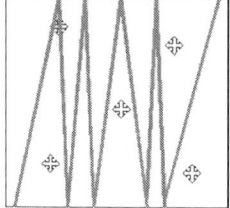

Random search: 20% of the time for 20% of the treasure (on average)

On the basis of your results, if you then decide to do a systematic search, you will spend **120% of the time for 100% of the finds**, so decide quickly to swap from a random search to a systematic one. If you are unlucky and miss all the treasure on a random search, do you write the site off as unproductive?

Or you could use dowsing to do this:

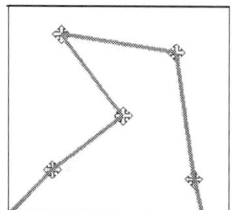

20% of the time for 100% of the finds (conservative estimate)

Clearly you could cover five times more sites in the time in takes to systematically search one site. **You should make at least five times more finds.** Let's see how we can do that...

5 FINDING AND USING A DOWSER

The object of this manual is really to show you how to dowse and then to use dowsing to help find *treasure*, whatever the word *treasure* may mean to you. Having said that, you may want the results without doing your own dowsing. Instead of, or as well as, learning to dowse, alternatives might be to find someone amongst your family or friends who would have a go or consult an amateur or professional dowser. I must admit that I chose the latter before I did any dowsing to speak of, as I wanted to see just what a dowser could achieve.

The advantage of using an accomplished dowser is that it is likely to be the most successful in the short term. There are disadvantages however:

*You will have to pay a modest fee or a percentage of your resulting finds.

*You may have to wait until the dowser can fit you in.

*If you don't ask the right questions to start with, you may not get useful information back.

Dowsers tend to specialise; most are interested in finding water. If water is your treasure, fine, find a water dowser. If you prefer your treasure more metallic then you need a dowser interested in finding metal. You wouldn't call a plumber to fix your television, after all. Occasionally dowsers advertise in the treasure hunting press and these dowsers are worth looking out for, because they probably have the right skills and interests. A quicker way of finding a suitable dowser is to contact your national Dowsing

Society. These societies are always very approachable and helpful since they exist mainly to promote dowsing and find work for their members. You will, of course, need to specify, in broad terms, what you want the dowser to do. For instance, what do you want the dowser to look for and do you want him to dowse a map or look for something out in the field. It's always worth trying to find a dowser near at hand even if you are only interested in having a map dowsed. You'll see later on that inaccuracies creep into map dowsing, which may only be overcome by dowsing on site. I can assure you that there is little as frustrating as being told where something desirable is buried and not being able to find it.

When you have found your dowser you will need to come to some arrangement to recompense them for their time and expenses. Some ask for a fee, others a percentage of the resulting recovery, it's up to you to negotiate, however I have always found that dowsers love to dowse and as a result they don't expect excessively high rewards. If you find a proficient dowser, you will get exceptional value for money and probably a good friend.

Jimmy Longton in action

6 THE PENDULUM

A pendulum can, in the hands of a good map dowser, pinpoint the position of anything buried; from a single coin to a lost city, many miles away. For the treasure hunter, this aspect of dowsing holds enormous potential for locating sites, regardless of their state of cultivation and without the need of permission. Further, once any necessary permission has been obtained, the same technique can be used to plot the treasure content of the site, facilitating rapid retrieval.

All you need to start is a pendulum, which is basically a weight on a line that acts as a little computer, moving in different ways according to the information you require:

*It will move in a circle in response to a buried or hidden object either over a map or out in the field.

*It may differentiate between objects; ferrous and non-ferrous for example, by gyrating clockwise for one type or anti clockwise for another.

*It will respond similarly to unambiguous questions phrased so that the answer ought to be only yes or no.

*It can indicate a direction by oscillation.

You can use many things found around the home to make a pendulum. Pendants, rings, fishing weights, hexagonal nuts, cotton reels or buttons all make perfectly acceptable pendulums.

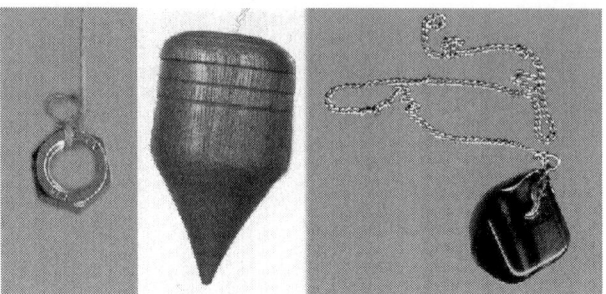

A simply made pendulum, a wood cavity pendulum and a quartz pendulum

There are a few points to consider, however:

*The nearer the shape of the weight is to a builder's plumb-bob, the better it will perform mechanically.

*Natural materials, such as wood or crystal for the weight and cotton or silk for the line, are claimed to be preferable to artificial materials. Having said that; many pendulums are made from brass – a man-made alloy!

*All things being equal, a favorite personal object or one of sentimental value will make a good pendulum. Professional dowser Jimmy Longton, used a cross he normally wore around his neck.

*You could use an object made from the same metal that you are seeking.

*Some dowsers prefer to use a cavity pendulum, which has a chamber to hold a sample of what you are looking for; a silver coin or gold coin can be dropped in, for instance.

*The larger the pendulum, the larger the circle it will describe. This is of little consequence for most uses but a large pendulum will be less accurate than a small one for pinpointing when used directly over a map.

*You can purchase ready-made pendulums from New Age stores or Dowsing Societies.

*You could ask a wood turner or a jeweler to make you one.

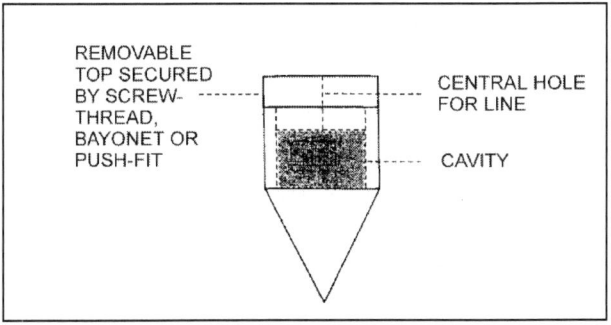

Cavity pendulum turned from hardwood, e.g. Beech. Dimensions are 2.5 x 1.25 inches (6.5cm x 3.25cm). NB. Avoid using metal in its construction or you may find only nails!

If you have any trouble deciding, just pick an object close to plumb-bob shape; once you have learned how to use the pendulum you can experiment with different objects and materials. When you have chosen your weight, assuming it is not already suspended, you need to fix a line to it. Cotton, wool, silk or sisal string will all do fine. The usual operating length of a pendulum line is about four inches (10cm); however, it is advisable to make the line around 10 inches (25cm) long to allow adjustment to find the best operating length for yourself. You can trim it down later if you wish but meanwhile just keep the excess out of the way of the moving weight. Bear in mind that longer lines allow the pendulum to describe larger circles and beware the advice of those who claim that success in locating gold, for instance, is dependent on the line length. A popular myth is that the line length required for finding gold is 44 inches (112cm). Try it by all means but you will probably find it unworkable as the pendulum not only tends to wrap itself around your leg but also you are too far away to clearly see the map you are trying to dowse.

The most popular way to hold the pendulum is to pinch the line, between your thumb and forefinger, as if the line is a pinch of salt to be sprinkled on food. Keep your thumb and forefinger still though, do not sprinkle. Another way of holding the pendulum is to hold your hand as a pretend pistol. Extend your forefinger and run the line over the top and down the back of your forefinger clamping it with your thumb, about an inch from the end of your finger. The way you hold the pendulum is unimportant providing the weight is free to move on the end of its line. The best way to hold the pendulum is the way that feels most comfortable to you.

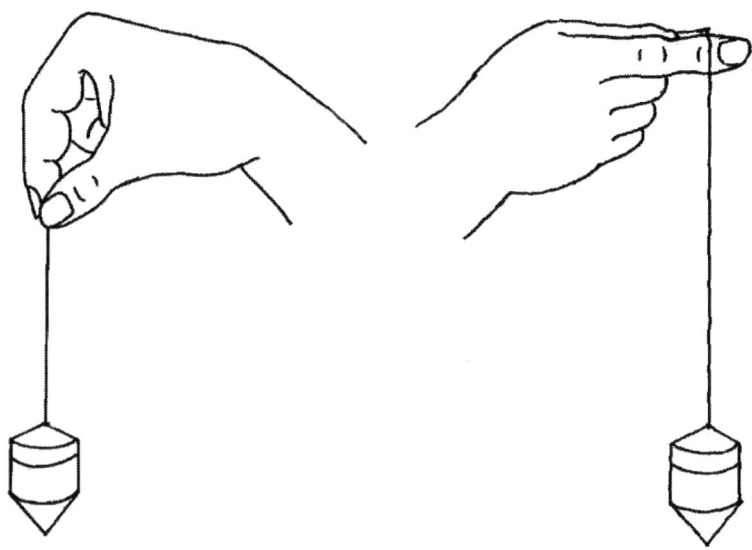

Pendulum responses vary from person to person. You will need to establish what your pendulum's responses mean to you by asking it some questions. Before we get to that I should say something about the strange idea of holding conversations with normally inanimate objects such as dowsing devices. The given advice is to talk to them as a pet, normally kindly but scold if necessary. To anyone who ever owned a pet rock this should present no problem. If you find talking out loud to your dowsing devices embarrassing, then just think your questions, it makes no difference. We come back to the point that I cannot emphasize enough — you must be comfortable with what you are doing.

As the pendulum cannot react instantly to a stimulus, it improves the response time if you apply a little force to keep the pendulum oscillating gently backwards and forwards in a rocking motion, towards you and away from you. This is called 'idling'.

With your pendulum idling, ask it to show you yes, no & don't know, in turn. Typically, the pendulum will circle clockwise for yes, anti-clockwise for no and oscillate in a straight line for don't know. If the pendulum won't respond or gives the same response regardless of what you ask, you will need to train it. Take a piece of blank paper and draw a circle about two inches (5cm) diameter then hold the pendulum above the circle and persuade the pendulum to follow the circle in both clockwise and anticlockwise directions. Cheat, if you must and physically force the pendulum to circle.

Draw a large cross (+) on the paper, mark the points North, South, East, West and orientate the paper as near as possible to the true compass points. Ask the pendulum to show you the points, one by one. If you get an identical response on opposite points, for example, North − South you can ask the pendulum to differentiate by saying something like "Is that North?" The pendulum's yes response would confirm North; the no response − South.

Here are a couple of exercises worth doing to help train yourself to use the pendulum:

Line up three, or more, upturned opaque cups and find someone to hide a coin beneath one of them, while you are out of the room. Hold your pendulum over each one in turn and ask: "Is there a coin beneath this cup?" When you frequently obtain a yes response over the cup with the coin under it, you are starting to get somewhere.

Here's one you can do on your own. Take a pack of playing cards, shuffle them and place them face down on a table in front of you. Hold the pendulum over the top card and ask "Is the top card a red card?" If the response is yes, remove the top card and place it on the table, face down, at the right of the pack; if no, place the card on the left. Repeat the exercise until you have gone through the entire pack. If you look at the right hand pile of cards they should be predominantly hearts and diamonds. Count the number of red cards and the total number of cards in the pile. Your percentage success rate can be calculated by dividing the reds by the total and multiplying by 100. Eg.16 reds in a total of 26 would be 62%, which is about my current success rate; not brilliant but a useful 12% better than random selection, which should improve with practice.

And finally a few comments on a couple of points I mentioned at the beginning of this chapter:

*You can train the pendulum to automatically distinguish between ferrous and non-ferrous metals when dowsing directly over a map if you find that useful but remember treasure was sometimes buried in iron containers. However, to do this you just have to ask the pendulum to show you ferrous metal and non-ferrous metal in turn, to determine which way your pendulum gyrates for the type of metal.

*The pendulum can be used to guide you to treasure out in the field by the direction of its oscillation. By that I mean the pendulum will oscillate in a direct line between you and the treasure you are seeking so you can just follow the direction of swing until you reach the treasure, when the pendulum will let you know by changing from oscillation into gyration. I don't personally find this so easy as using an L-rod which we will be covering in chapter 8, however if it suits you, it is another option.

7 MAP DOWSING

The first thing you need to do when map dowsing is to decide what you want to find. Are you looking for productive sites, a cache (hoard) or individual coins and artifacts? You will need to select or scale your map according to the size of your target. You wouldn't expect to pinpoint a single coin on a map of an entire county any more than locate a deserted medieval village on a plan of your back garden. For dowsing caches or individual artifacts you need to use a 1:1267 (50 inches to one mile; 79cm to 1km) scale or larger. For dowsing sites, 1:10560 (6 inches to one mile; 9.5cm to 1km) is ideal. If you haven't a map of the right scale, you can adjust it easily by either enlarging or reducing, using a photocopier or a pantograph drawing device. Aim to have the final map around A4 size (297mm x 210mm or 12" x 8").

As usual, there is more than one way to dowse a map and you can use a pendulum or a single L-rod, which will swing to indicate a target or response to a question. The traditional way, using a pendulum, is to comfortably position yourself over the map, sitting, kneeling or standing. With the pendulum idling, very slowly move it over the map systematically, while concentrating on what you wish to find. Every time the pendulum gyrates, mark a cross on the map as near as you can to the centre of the circle that the pendulum is describing. You will find it helpful, for eventual recovery, if you mark on the map the direction of pendulum travel, since pinpointing is usually somewhat off target in that direction. The reason for this is that it takes time for the pendulum to start gyrating in order to indicate a target; meanwhile the pendulum is still being moved forward. If you take four minutes to cover one mile on the map, relatively speaking, the pendulum is travelling at 15 mph. Imagine running a four-minute mile across a field, while trying to spot a coin dropped somewhere on the surface. Even if you manage to see the coin, by the time you have realized and stopped, the coin will be some way behind you.

The map dowsing method I prefer uses a fine grid to divide the map into manageable sectors of rows and columns. An easy way to put a suitable grid onto the map is to photocopy a quadrille ruled (one quarter inch or 5mm squares) sheet of paper onto an A4 copy of the map. Better still, you will get the grid on the map in one pass, if you photocopy the quadrille ruling onto a clear acetate sheet, and then photocopy your maps through the acetate. If you haven't got access to a photocopier and don't want to pay the library or print store for photocopying, you can simply draw a grid on your map with a pencil and ruler.

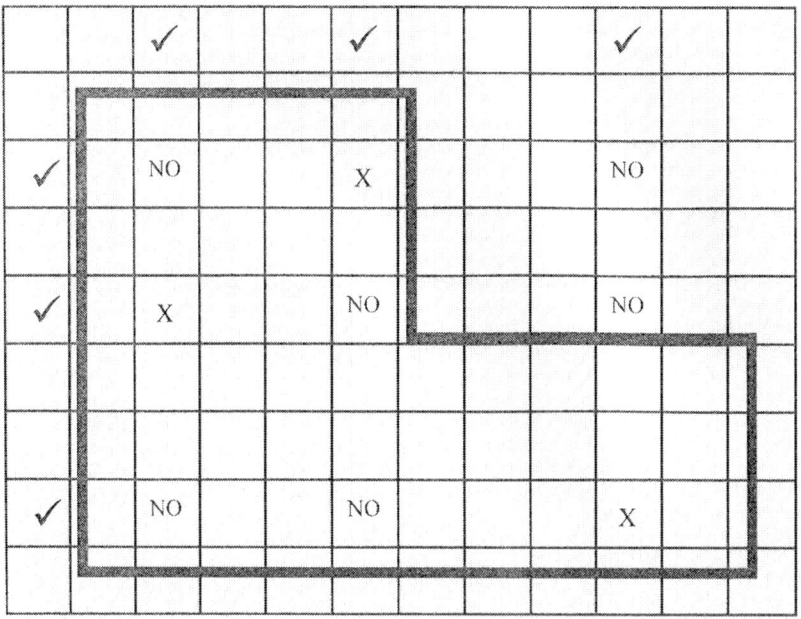

To dowse the map simply point with a pencil or pen at one end of each row in turn and with either the pendulum or L-rod in your other hand, ask: 'Is there any treasure in this row?' I use the word treasure, for an unspecified desirable metal object. Feel free to ask for whatever you want to find by any name you choose, as long as it means something to you. Every time you get a yes response from your dowsing tool, place a tick at the end of the appropriate row. When you have checked all the rows, repeat the exercise with each column. If there is only one treasure on your map it will be located at the intersection of your ticked row and your ticked column. You will probably have more than one treasure on your map, which will involve a little more questioning of your dowsing tool. If you have three ticked rows and three ticked columns, then you have nine possible treasure locations, each at the intersection of every ticked row with every ticked column. To sort the real from the possible, you point to each intersection in turn and ask: 'Is there treasure buried here?' Mark all your yes responses and there you have it.

There is another map dowsing method particularly useful in looking for a single treasure. This is more suitable for the L-rod although the pendulum can be used with slightly less accuracy. You need a ruler for this one, a rolling ruler preferably and a writing implement. All you do is to slowly move the ruler across the map asking your L-rod or pendulum to indicate when the leading edge of the ruler meets the treasure you seek. When the rod swings or the pendulum gyrates you stop moving the ruler and draw a line on the map along the leading edge of the ruler. Turn the ruler through 90° so that it is across the line you have just drawn and, starting at one end of the line, run the ruler slowly along it while asking for the treasure on the leading edge. Again, when your L-rod or pendulum indicates, stop moving the ruler and draw another line down the ruler's leading edge. Your treasure is located at the intersection of the two lines.

Whichever way you dowse the map, if you want more information about the targets you have dowsed such as what metal it is, how deep or how old, you only have to ask your pendulum or L-rod. Remember though that whichever tool you use it can only answer yes or no, so you need to phrase your questions carefully. For determining the metal you would just ask in turn: 'Is this treasure made of gold?' 'Is it made of silver?' Etc. For depth you would ask questions like: 'Is it more than three feet deep?' 'Is it less than two feet deep?' Then, assuming you had a no to both: 'Is it 24 inches deep?' Is it 25 inches deep?' And so on until you hit a yes.

All you have to do now is to find your targets and dig them. I don't know why it happens but even if you use the most accurate surveying equipment money can buy to translate the cross on your map onto mother earth; there is a good chance that pinpointing will not be exact! For example, on a six-inch Ordnance Survey map Jimmy Longton dowsed for me, he identified six targets, five of which I have probably found. However, the distance between the targets on the map and the actual targets varied between zero and 220 meters. Based on the worst error, the remaining target lies somewhere in a circle 440 meters in diameter, which takes in all or part of eight fields in various states of cultivation. Five fields belong to one landowner; three to another. You can appreciate the problem.

Another dowser friend, Frank Delamere dowsed photographs of a treasure site with excellent results in that investigating Frank's predicted locations on the photographs I recovered a greater number of gold coins than had been found previously. I can only say that using a photograph instead of a map (Frank was 100 meters out when he dowsed a map of the site) seems a lot more accurate and well worth the extra effort involved in taking the photograph.

Unless you just want to trust to luck that by searching in the right general area you may stumble across the target, the best way to successful recovery is to use dowsing rods. The best dowsers can stand at the field gate and ask the rods to show them where a particular target is buried, walk over to it and dig it up. The rest of us have to work a bit harder. Nevertheless, if you use your rods as described in the previous chapter, in the places dowsed on your maps or photographs, you may soon be recovering more treasure than you thought possible.

I'll just finish this chapter by mentioning Jerry Nokes. Jerry has developed a method of map dowsing which basically involves a simple method of tracking the target. You need to know where the target originated to get a starting point and providing you know that, then this method will lead you to where the target is now. You could for instance track king John's baggage train to its sinking in the Wash or a shipwreck from the port the ship sailed from. Jerry has produced an Internet course which you can check out here: http://map-dowsing-is-obsolete.com/index.html

8 THE L-ROD

While, as a generalization, all dowsing tools can be used for all types of dowsing, the pendulum is best used for map dowsing and the L-rod for field dowsing. The basic L-rod is simply a length of stiff metal wire or thin round bar bent into the shape of the letter 'L', hence the name, although some might argue that it is an abbreviation of Locator Rod. Traditionally the short arm of the 'L' is held in a loose fist while the long arm projects forward over the top of the fist. There are a few variations on the basic design and my personal preference is an inverted model that Jimmy Longton used and kindly allowed me to reproduce here. If you already have a pair of L-rods you are happy with, by all means use them or you can make excellent rods as follows:

You will need 22 inches (56cm) of round metal bar (brass is considered best) of one-sixteenth inch (1.5mm) to three-sixteenths inch (5mm) in diameter to make each rod. Unless you have easy access to round bar, I suggest you use two wire clothes hangers. (NB Measurements and angles do not need to be too precise to make a working rod):

1. Invert the first hanger and measure 14 inches (36cm) from one side, along the horizontal bar then mark and cut through with a pair of pliers or a junior hacksaw. Measure 22 inches (56cm) back from the first cut and make a second cut. Discard the hooked portion.

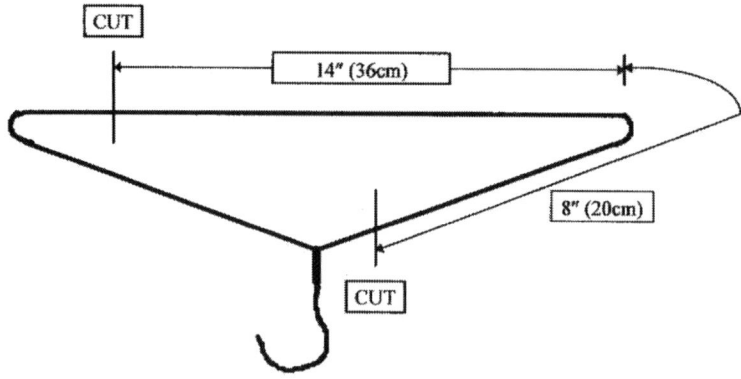

2. Smooth the cut ends with a file or emery cloth. Using a pair of pliers or a vice, first straighten and then bend the shorter arm back to an angle of 135°.

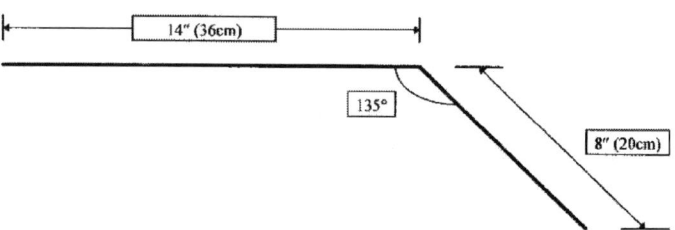

3. From the cut end, measure seven inches (18cm) along the shorter arm, and bend this back until horizontal.

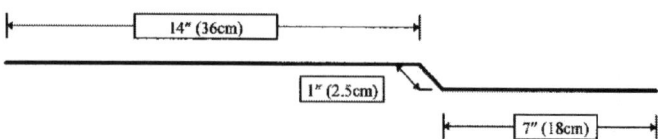

4. Turn the last five and a half inches (14cm) up at right angles, and then turn the last half inch (1cm) of the upright inwards, at right angles.

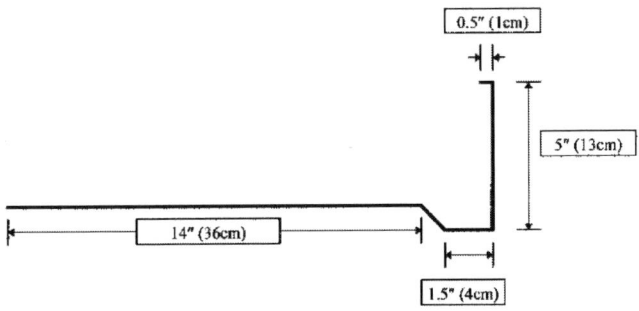

5. Lay the rod on a level surface and adjust it until it lies reasonably flat.

6. Make a second rod from the other coat hanger.

Health warning: The rods are perfectly harmless when used as described. If you wish to use them to play Conan the Barbarian, Robin Hood, Ivanhoe or act out any other fantasy, don't blame me if you puncture your eyeball or any other part of your body. I would suggest that children using the rods should be supervised by a responsible adult. The rods can be made extra safe by folding their tips downwards or back on themselves, wrapping their tips with insulating tape or applying a blob of a resin such as Araldite.

Take the short arm of a rod in each hand so that the long arm is on the opposite side to your thumbs. Clench your fists around them loosely and turn your wrists so that your thumbs are uppermost and the long arm projects forward from the bottom of your fist. Tuck your elbows into your body and keep your upper arms in line with your body. Hold your forearms straight out in front of you, the width of your body apart and at whatever angle necessary to keep the rods reasonably parallel to the ground. (The rods tend to naturally point slightly downward towards the ground, which is fine.) The rods should now be pointing forward like extensions of your forearms. You may need to adjust your grip so that the rods are just free to move but not sloppy. When you are happy with holding the rods we can move on to some dowsing exercises.

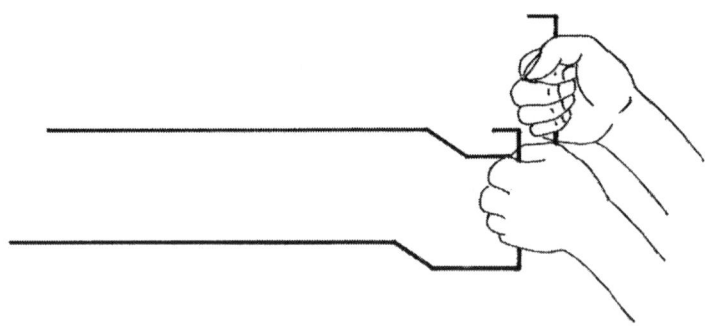

Holding the rods

1. Hold the rods in the normal dowsing position as just described. Ask the rods to turn left. After they have moved, restart the rods pointing forward. The easy way to get the rods to point forward is to drop your forearms so that the rods point to the ground then raise your forearms back to the horizontal. Ask the rods to turn right. Restart. Ask the rods to cross. The rods will cross on your chest. Practice until the rods move easily.

2. Place a coin on the floor then take a few paces back from it. Hold your rods in the normal dowsing position and walk slowly toward the coin saying: 'I am looking for a coin'. The rods will either cross as you pass immediately over the coin or within a few paces past the coin. Keep practicing until the rods cross at the coin.

3. Place a copper coin; a silver coin and a brass coin some distance apart on the ground. Hold your rods in the normal dowsing position and walk slowly toward the coin saying: 'I am looking for a copper coin'. The rods will cross as you pass over the copper coin but not the other two. Repeat the exercise looking for a silver coin and then looking for a brass coin. Keep practicing until you can differentiate between various metals.

4. Stand sideways to a distant building or other large object that you know the location of and ask the rods to show you where it is. Give the full name of the place, i.e. 'Show me St. James' Church'. Clear your mind of everything else and concentrate. Once you get this to work, try standing with your back to the 'target' and see what happens.

5. When you have succeeded with exercise (4), take your rods to the gate of

a field or any other open space where you have any necessary search permission. Hold the rods as normal and ask: 'are there any coins buried in this field?' Normally the rods will cross for yes and move apart or open out for no. As with the pendulum you may need to determine what the rods' movement, or lack of it, means for you. Ask the rods to point to the nearest coin, then walk slowly in the direction indicated by the rods, turning, as necessary, to keep the rods pointing straight out in front of you. On reaching the coin the rods will cross. If you want to search for other objects as well as coins, ask the rods to find 'treasure'.

Keep practicing. Once you can obtain a response from the rods in all these exercises, you are basically ready to do anything. Even if you can't do it all at first, you should find that the rods will produce some useful results in the field and you will improve with time.

You may have noticed that in exercise (5) you located your first buried treasure but how do you recover it? It is almost essential to use a metal detector for final location of metallic objects, as pinpointing by dowsing alone is rarely precise. If you are looking for non-metallic treasures than that is a different ball game and unless you can devise your own pinpointing technique, presumably you are just going to have to dig for it. Returning to exercise (5), using two rods leaves you no hands free to carry anything so, hopefully you will have brought someone else along, who can, at least, carry a metal detector and extraction tool, and perhaps do the digging for you. If you are the independent sort, you don't need to have a partner, it's very easy to both dowse and recover targets by yourself using a metal detector and one of the following methods.

1. Dowse and mark first, detect and dig second. You will need a couple of dozen 24 inch (60cm) long pea sticks from a garden centre and something in which to carry them on your back or hip. I use an archery quiver but I am sure most of you could make or adapt something for carrying the sticks if you wanted to save some money. All you do then is dowse and mark where the rods cross by pushing a stick into the ground. When you run out of sticks, set your detector up and detect from stick to stick, collecting the sticks as you go, as well as the finds.

2. You can dowse with just one rod, believe it or not. The great advantage with single rod dowsing is that you have one hand free to use a metal detector, so you can both dowse and detect simultaneously. All you have to do is to sweep with the detector using one hand while holding the rod in your other hand. To recover what you detect you only have to find a means of carrying a digging tool, without using your hands.

Small digging implements can be carried in a finds bag and for a long time I carried a 'T' handled foot assisted trowel on a tool belt, which has worked well. But now metal detectors go deeper than in the past, it has become necessary to use a small spade. I use a Draper Mini Spade with D Handle. The digger is 28 inches (72cm) long and has a rounded point hardened steel blade with foot bars. The high strength Glass fiber shaft makes it extremely strong yet light, weighing two pounds or slightly under a kilogram. Now I can drag this spade along by fitting a quick release loop through the D handle and attaching that to a tool belt. That's fine on a beach, grass or bare earth; it even leaves a trail so you can see where you've been. But if, like me, you search among growing crops, the crop is likely to be damaged and the farmer won't be happy. So I needed to carry the spade without it contacting the ground.

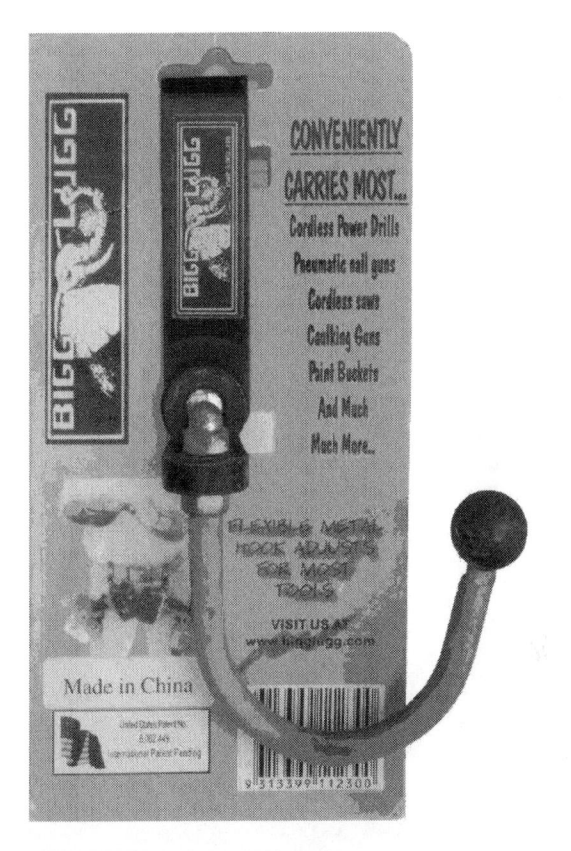

I discovered the Bigg Lugg belt hook, above, which after some experimenting has proved to be the ideal solution. (An alternative is the McGuire-Nicholas 93333 Monster Hook Cordless Drill Holder Holster Belt Clip.) First I used the hook on my trouser or pants waist belt on the opposite side to my detector. The problem with that was that the spade acted like a pendulum and kept swinging too close to the detector head and causing a signal. I then remembered, Phil, a detectorist who sadly had lost one arm in a motorcycle accident. Phil used a belt hook to carry his spade behind him, although I didn't realize at the time why he carried his spade in that position. Once I moved the hook round to the rear, searching became nice and silent once more (until I hit a target, that is). A bonus was that if I moved too fast the spade tapped on the back of my legs to remind me to slow down. Another slight problem remained, which was the weight of the spade on my waist belt made my trousers or pants slip downward. Having to adjust my attire frequently was a nuisance. I resolved that one by using a separate dedicated belt for hook and spade. So I can now dowse and detect simultaneously on any terrain with no distractions.

While we are on the subject of recovery, I ought to mention some of the pitfalls. A metal detector will not be able to detect every target that you dowse. Dowsing goes far deeper than metal detectors. I have heard of match-head sized silver objects, dowsed at depths of three feet and I have dowsed targets that only produced a signal from a detector after I had dug out 12 inches (30cm) depth of soil first. You can, of course, just dig a hole wherever your rods indicate a target but, unless you are looking for something specific like a suspected hoard or cache, you are likely to find this approach counter-productive as it could take a couple of hours to dig each hole. I fit the largest suitable search-head to my detector; if a search for a target doesn't produce a signal, I just leave it and go on to the next target. I couldn't have found the target anyway, had I only used a detector.

Recently disturbed ground can be quite frustrating to dowse owing to a phenomenon called remanence. When an object is removed from the ground, dowsing rods still react to the spot where it lay for about a fortnight, in my experience. Conversely, when an object is placed in the ground it takes a similar amount of time before rods will react to it. Beware freshly ploughed fields, detecting rallies and the dry sands of beaches in summer!

So far as search techniques are concerned there are several approaches depending on the type of site and your temperament.

* Theoretically you should be able to just follow the rods or rod from one good target to the next, by moving your body to keep your forearm(s) in line with the rod(s). This is probably the easiest way and it is excellent for checking out a site for the first time. However, unless you are really good at discriminating you may miss some desirable targets.

* There is a more systematic approach for dowsing with two rods and one that is almost essential for searching sites like orchards or woodland, where you are unable to walk around unrestricted. Search in straight lines about two meters or two yards apart; the rods will cross if you walk over a target or there is a target to the left or right of you. Just put a stick in the ground at your feet as a marker whenever the rods cross. When you come to look for the target you need to detect a circle around your marker at least twice the width between your search lines. Your detecting area should be four meters (or four yards) in diameter if your search lines are two meters (or two yards) apart. If you are searching an orchard, for example, there is no need to fight your way through the trees trying to detect for targets which you suspect lie in the next row. You can deal with such targets when you come to search that row. If you are searching open land it will help to define your detecting areas if you leave your markers in place until you have finished recovering targets. You should then end up having lines of markers to follow in place of the natural lines, formed by the trees in an orchard (Fig. 1).

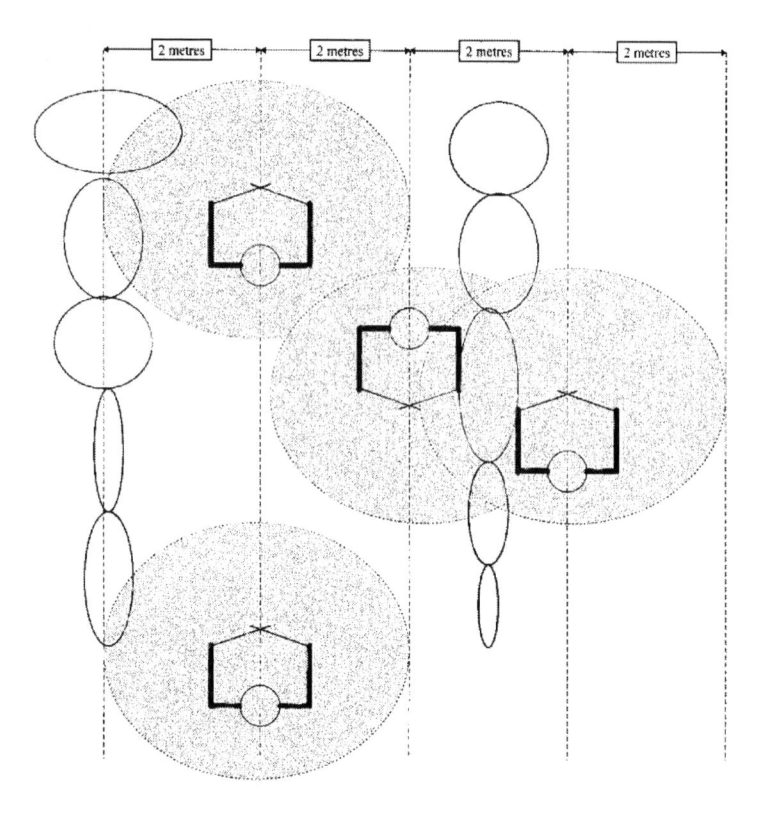

Fig 1: Systematic dowsing with two rods. Detect shaded areas.

* You can improve on this two-rod method a little by making the initial target location a two-stage process. Every time your rods cross, restart the rods and ask them to point at the target. Then, when you push your marker stick into the ground, lean it in the direction indicated by the rods. That will halve the search area as you only need to detect on the left side or the right side of the marker, depending on which way it is leaning.

* I find systematic dowsing with a single rod easier than using two rods since the single rod actually points at the target to tell you there is something there. Also a single rod is less sensitive than two, which helps reduce the amount of less desirable targets and automatically you are given a more precise target location. For orchards and the like, search in straight lines as with two rods; as you approach a target the, rod will start to turn. Walk slowly on until the rod is just pointing behind you, by which time you

will probably have lost control of it and it will be resting against your arm. Put a marker in at your feet, leaning it to the left if the rod turned left or to the right if the rod turned right. Walk forward a couple of paces so that you are well clear of the target, then turn yourself around 180 degrees so that you are facing the way you have just come. Restart the rod and retrace your steps slowly past your marker until the rod turns to point behind you once again. Place another marker leaning to the side the rod pointed. You should now have two markers, leaning in the same direction which, theoretically, form the two ends of the base line of a triangle with the target lying at the apex. There is no need to worry about the trigonometry. When you return with your metal detector, just search all the area between the two markers and from the markers out to the tree line. (Fig. 2)

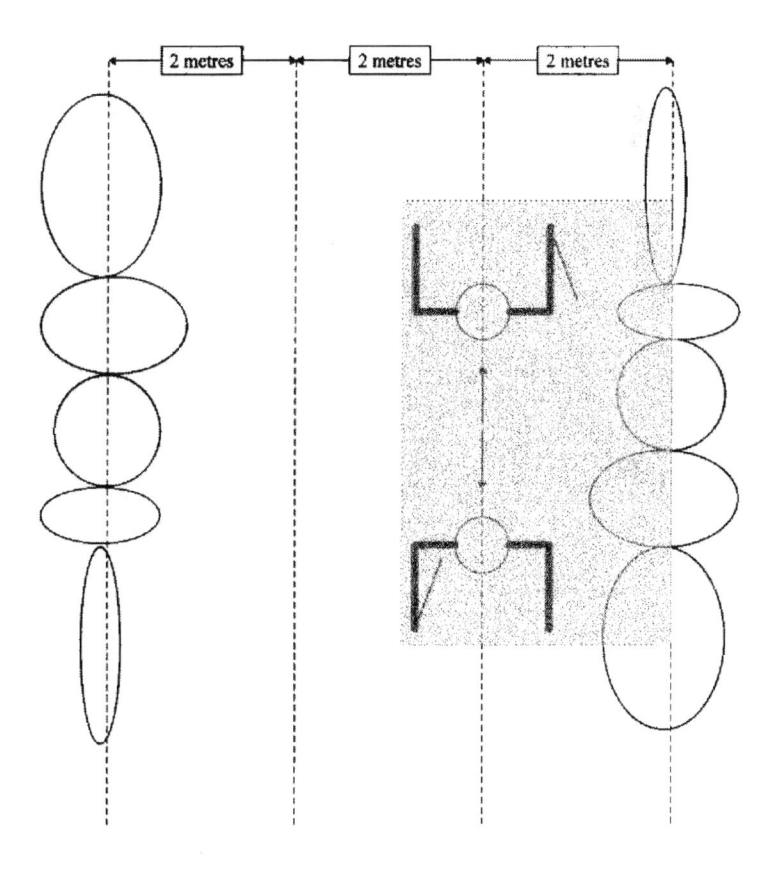

Fig 2: Dowsing between trees etc. with a single rod. Detect shaded area.

* For searching open land with a single rod you can use the "boxing-in" method. If you also carry a metal detector you only need half a dozen small marker sticks that you could carry in your finds pouch. Search in lines two meters (or two yards) apart as before. When the rod starts to turn, keep walking until the rod is pointing behind you (as in Fig. 2). Put down a marker, turn yourself 90 degrees in the direction that the rod pointed, back off a couple of paces so that the rod isn't influenced immediately by the target, restart the rod and walk slowly on until it turns again to the same side as previously. Put down another marker. Repeat the process twice more and you should then have four markers in the ground with each marker forming a corner of a rectangle or box. Theoretically the target will lie at the centre of the box but detect the entire area of the box in case there is more than one target. (Fig. 3).

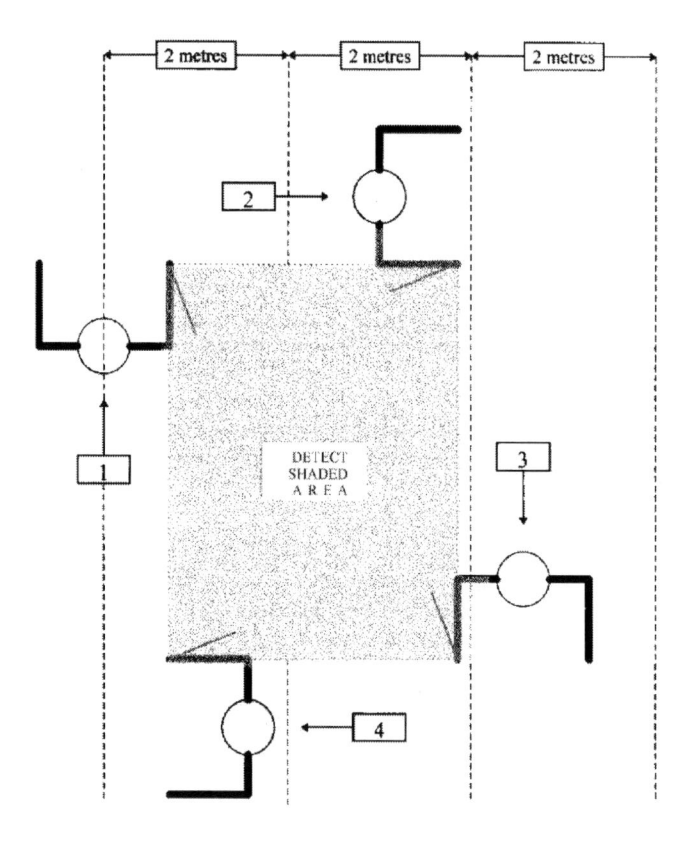

Fig 3: The 'boxing-in' method

In the last two methods, you will quite often find that after you've placed a marker, your rod unexpectedly swings to the "wrong" side. This is caused by there being two or more targets in close proximity. When this happens, place a marker; restart the rod and continue walking until the rod swings to the "correct" side then place another marker. When you have finished marking the first target, you can go back to the "out of place" marker and dowse for the second target.

There is a further method called 'intersecting', which is particularly good for locating a single larger target such as a cache. Hold the rod and once it is steady, note the direction it is pointing, and then mark the direction with a straight piece of wood. Move about ten paces to one side and repeat the process. If you run a line out in the marked direction, from each point; the target lies where both lines cross.

An easier way is to make up two 48 inch (120cm) timber laths of approx. one inch (2.5cm) square section, drill a hole of about one quarter inch (6mm) diameter in the end of each lath, thread with strong string and secure. Take your laths out to your site and from your starting point, get your rod to point at the target, and then follow the rod towards the target, dragging one lath behind you by the string, with your free hand. When the rod swings around, drop the lath and return to your starting point, where you should have left your other lath. Pick up the lath and move about ten paces to the left or right, then get your rod to point at the target again and follow your rod towards the target dragging the lath. Most of the time you will arrive at the point you dropped your first lath, the rod will swing and you drop your second lath on top of the first. The target should lie where the laths cross. (Fig. 4)

Sometimes the rod will react to a different target, before you reach the one where you dropped the first lath. In that case it is a good idea to mark the second target, and then get your rod to point in the direction you were travelling again and make a further "run" with the lath to establish the first target. Once you have sorted the first target. You can repeat the process to locate other targets.

Fig 4: Modified 'intersecting' method

9 TO BAIT OR NOT TO BAIT

While, for obvious reasons, there is much secrecy in treasure hunting, now and again you come across someone who willingly shares their knowledge, expertise and even their equipment! Takis, from Greece, is just such a person (and not the only one I might add) and his generosity has instigated a step change in my dowsing and treasure pursuits. "I have seventy dowsing books and this is the best." He said, pointing me to **Dowsing for Treasure** (1984) by Russ Simmons.

Again with Takis' help, I got hold of a copy of the book, read, re-read and digested the contents. The greatest insight for me was the principle of using bait, a sample or witness to aid what you want to find. I had paid little attention to this because my dowsing mentor, Jimmy Longton, was such a good dowser he used a basically plain rod, having no need for accessories. I had thought of the possibility of adding a sample chamber to an L-rod but had taken it no further. The reason being just using a dowsing rod in one hand and metal detector in the other achieved much better results than using a metal detector alone. If it is not broke, why fix it? Well you live and learn!

"I will make you dowsing rods like I use." Insisted Takis. I didn't argue as dowsing instruments are always special when received as an unsolicited gift. And soon two dowsing rods arrived in the mail…

The above picture shows one of the L-rods based on a pair that Takis sent me. I have digitally shortened the rod to fit in the photograph. Actual dimensions are: length 21 inches (52cm), height six inches (15cm) and return or short arm three inches (8cm). The diameter of the rod is one-sixteenth inch (1mm) and the sleeve handle three-eighths inch (6mm) outside diameter; one-quarter inch (4mm) internal. The only metal (alloy) used in construction is brass. The sample or bait container is a 2ml plastic test tube with screw cap. In the original version above, the tube sat in a short length of foam tubing attached to the back of a self adhesive hook plate. However, in the damp British climate, the adhesive bond kept failing so the sample tube now sits horizontally on the rod secured with two rubber 'O' rings or grommets.

The rod can be used either way up. I prefer to use it with the long arm below the hand as shown above. Takis prefers the rod the other way up, with the long arm above the hand.

The bait tube contains either a nominally pure sample or a duplicate of the metal or substance you seek. For instance, as I am interested in looking for Iron Age gold coins, Takis said I should grind a gold stater coin up to fit in the tube. I refused to do that and the alloy mix in ancient coins varies anyway, so I stick to pure metal samples, which you can buy on Ebay.

Because of the swivel handle, I expected the rod to be very sensitive and fly around all over the place but I was pleasantly surprised at its stability. It is even stable in windy conditions, which is probably a result of the thin rod used in construction.

I had a small pasture field available, which I had searched in the past and made few finds. The field had just been mown, so searching conditions were as good as they could be and I used the field as a test site for natural finds. I was now using a Detech EDS metal detector, fitted with 12 inch SEF coil, which I had not used on this field before. I baited the rod with silver and used the rod in one hand and detector in the other. Remember the brass (copper-zinc alloy) rod forms the largest sample or bait, so the rod will naturally find copper-alloys and should find silver because of the added silver bait. There may also be chance finds you just happen to walk over.

The photo above shows the finds made after a four hour search (plus there were three lead objects I couldn't fit into the photo). On the top row all seven objects are silver or silver-plate (the two George V sixpences are 50% silver). Old lead objects often contain traces of silver as an impurity. All other coins and artefacts in the photo are copper-alloy. There was also a little junk iron and aluminum.

A week later I changed the bait to gold on the L-rod and spent a further four hours detecting on the same field I used for the silver test. The photo below illustrates the finds. The first three objects from the left on the top row all have gold plating remaining while the fourth object is silver-plated copper-alloy. All remaining finds are copper-alloy. There was some junk in the form of iron and aluminum again, although this was minimal.

I admit this is not a very scientific test because every time a find is removed from the ground, the conditions of the experiment are changed. You can see this from the number of finds in the gold test dropping to a third compared to the silver test, for the same amount of detecting time. The law of diminishing returns in action! What is significant though is that in both the silver test and the gold test around one quarter of the finds contained the metal used for bait. If that continues in the field then, I am sure you will agree it must make a big difference to treasure hunting success…

10 BUILDING A BETTER GOLD TRAP

From what I learned from the experiments with the baited rod, plus good advice from another treasure dowser called David, I modified the original dowsing rod. If you want to follow my lead and you used steel clothes hanger wire for your rods, then you will need to start over making new rods, or a rod, as you only need one. There is a school of thought that stainless steel is good but I am convinced that it will attract rusty iron. I consider copper-alloy such as brass or bronze to be the best. I remade my rod using one-eighth inch (2mm) brass rod. The brass tube sleeve handle is four and three quarters inches (12cm) long, three-eighths inch (6mm) outside diameter; one-quarter inch (4mm) internal and the ends need to be smoothed with a file or emery cloth so that the rod can swing freely within the sleeve. If you are fitting the sleeve to an existing rod you should be able to straighten out the half-inch (1cm) stop and re-fix it after adding the sleeve. On David's advice I moved the sample or bait tube along to the tip of the rod for improved leverage. The attraction force can pull the rod around from the end more easily than from just in front of the handle.

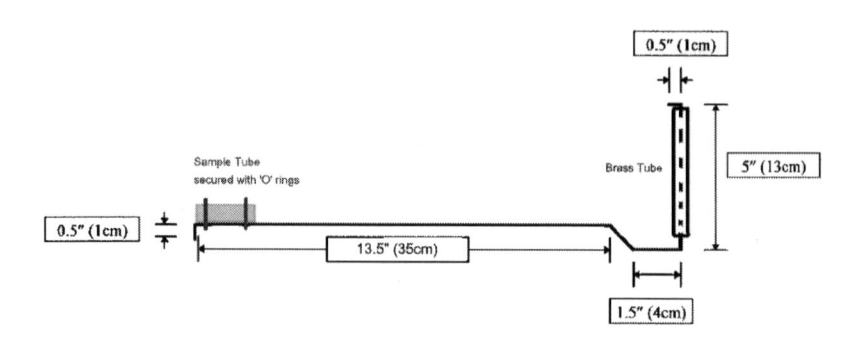

Modified Dowsing Rod

11 TO LOOK FOR OR TO UNLOOK FOR

What do you say or think to yourself when dowsing. Are you looking or unlooking?

Gold Eagle mount from the Staffordshire Anglo-Saxon hoard by Jon Callas, San Jose, USA [CC BY 2.0 (http://creativecommons.org/licenses/by/2.0)], via Wikimedia Commons.

Terry Herbert, finder of the Staffordshire hoard, the largest cache of Anglo-Saxon treasure ever found, said that, when detecting, he used the mantra: "Spirits of yesteryears take me where the treasure appears." He added that on the day that he found the first pieces of the cache, for reasons unknown, he substituted the word 'gold' for treasure in his mantra. It works for some!

Looking for something is easy, unlooking is not so easy. Try not thinking of an elephant! You need to think about something to not think about it.

I came across a modified Hawaiian ho'oponopono clearing technique, which Dr Ihaleakala Hew Len, a psychotherapist, claims cured criminally insane prisoners. Dr Len and Dr Joe Vitale (who features in **The Secret** film and book by Rhonda Byrne) discuss ho'oponopono in their book, **Zero Limits**. An audio book, **The Missing Secret**, by Joe Vitale also covers the technique in depth. You only have to constantly repeat the phrases: "I'm sorry. Please forgive me. Thank you. I love you." In any order you choose and you need not say it out loud. I know, logically, it sounds as if one of Dr Len's patients thought this up but I tried Terry Herbert's mantra and I get the best results from Dr Lens' mantra. It may simply be a technique to block our conscious mind to allow the subconscious to work or there may be more to it. We don't know everything! Use whatever works for you.

12 BUYING A BETTER GOLD TRAP

My gold and silver finds definitely increased using the baited dowsing rod. Then Takis said what I needed was a vintage Anderson (Precision Mineral Rod) PMR-II. This wasn't the first time I had been told this. In 2010 I had dowsing and treasure hunting lessons from Jerry Nokes who clearly regarded the Anderson rod as the best thing since sliced bread! Jerry said that he had bought one in 1977 and it had almost dragged him across a field to a treasure target. Swapping to the alternative spring handle, he dug up the target without even needing to use a metal detector. Praise indeed!

Now Takis, Jerry and many others were saying you have to get an older model made by Carl Anderson, the inventor, as the formula for the crystal charge installed in the rod died with him. The Anderson PMR-II is still made today by Carl Anderson's son-in-law, Russ Simmons, who wrote the book, **Dowsing for Treasure**, which started my interest in baited dowsing rods. The cut-off point is 2003, according to Jerry, presumably when Carl Anderson died. Now these rods are still being made and sold today, although more commonly called Universal Antenna Rods, so they have stood the test of time and the lost secret formula may just be an urban myth. Nevertheless I went with the given advice and on the third attempt bought a vintage Anderson PMR-II on Ebay, from the USA, for around $400.

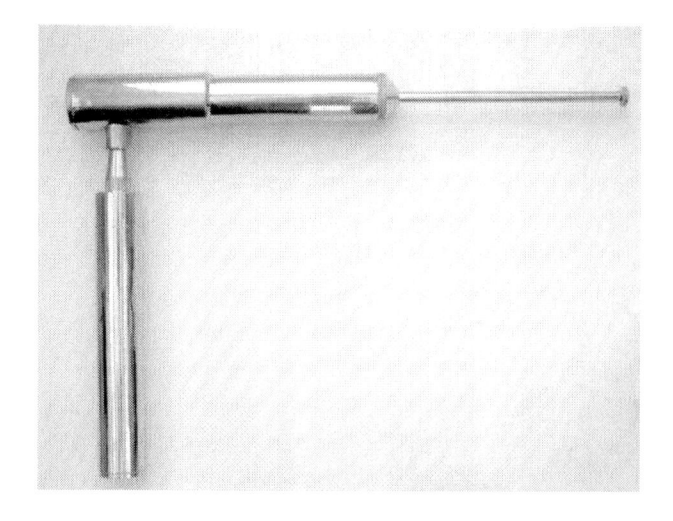

Anderson PMR II fitted with single-handed bearing handle

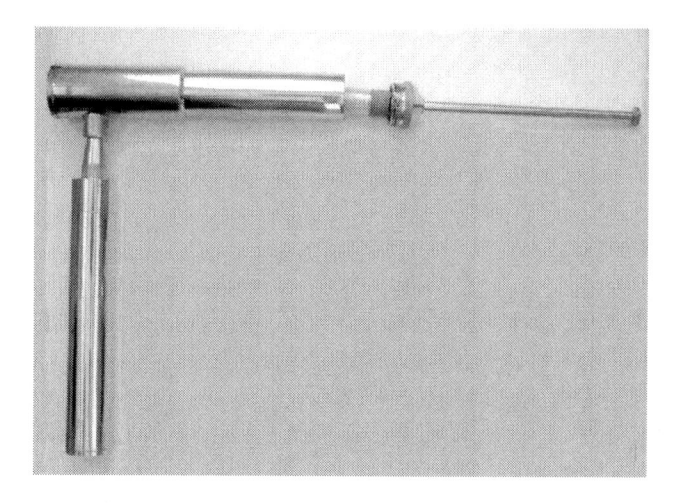

Anderson with the bait chamber cap unscrewed and silver bait showing

The Anderson PMR-II consists of a main tubular body, pre-charged with slightly radioactive crystals, according to the instruction sheet. There is a bait chamber behind a removable cap. You can use the rod without bait but the main idea is to put a sample of gold, silver or whatever you are looking for, in the chamber. So that you do not contaminate the chamber with traces of different samples, it is important to have the sample sealed in a plastic container. An adjustable antenna attaches to and extends from the body, while a variety of handles can be attached at right angles or in line with the body. I only had two handles at the time, a single-handed bearing handle, which makes the Anderson PMR-II work like an L-rod and a spring handle, which converts the device to a pendulum. The spring handle screws into the rear of the sample chamber, while the single-handed bearing handle is removed. Kybob has since kindly given me a 24-inch fibre handle, which completes the available handle options apart from the two-hand bearing handle. The fiber handle screws into the rear of the sample chamber, like the spring handle, and converts the device to a 'Y'-Rod, which, like its precursor, the forked-twig, requires the use of both hands to operate.

First impressions were that the device is well constructed and handles well. To familiarize myself, I started by using the PMR-II as an L-rod, without the antenna extended as advised by Takis. I marked the targets the rod indicated and retrieved them later using a metal detector and spade. While I did find some buttons plated with gold or silver, like the sample in the chamber, I also found a lot of iron! Would it work better if I used the Anderson PMR-II in one hand and metal detector in the other as I did with the L-rod?

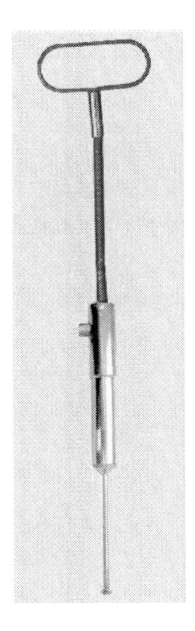

Anderson PMR-II with spring handle

13 ALL THAT GLITTERS

Gold plated buttons

Using the Anderson PMR-II rod, fitted with the single-handed bearing handle, in one hand and my detector in the other worked well. I had absolutely no issues balancing the Anderson; its weight seems to keep it stable. What to do with the Anderson PMR-II when I needed to dig was an issue at first. I started by carrying a cloth to lay the Anderson on, when I put it on the ground, but that became a chore. Then I discovered that the Anderson could be rested across the handle and against the control box of my Detech EDS detector and would sit there when I was holding my detector while digging. I keep my hand on the Anderson PMR-II though as should it fall it may damage the antenna. The antenna is replaceable but would involve buying and importing a new one from the manufacturer. If the digging gets tough and I need to lie my detector down, I found that the Anderson will rest in the detector's arm cup.

So I started by baiting the Anderson with silver which worked well. I found silver coins and silver-plated objects as well as copper-alloy (the Anderson is constructed of chromium plated brass, I believe) and lead (old lead contains silver as an impurity). So far so good!

I then baited the Anderson PMR-II with gold, which I expected to turn up gold coins but that did not happen. Over the past 200 years many fields in the south of England, where I live, have been fertilized with rag waste contaminated with buttons and other metal objects associated with clothing. The Anderson PMR-II took a great liking to gold plated buttons (as in picture) and similar objects as well as copper-alloys. I guess this is because I was using almost pure gold bait and gold plating comprises high karat gold, a perfect match to the Anderson.

I was hoping to find Iron Age gold stater coins which have a variable mix of gold (70-80%), silver (10-20%) and copper (5-10%). This is a moving target so even using a gold coin as bait there would be no guarantee of matching the coins in the field. I could persevere with the gold bait or because most, particular older, man-made gold objects contain either silver or copper or both I could switch back to silver bait...

Then it started to happen, with the Anderson PMR-II baited with pure silver, I found two gold coins on separate occasions.

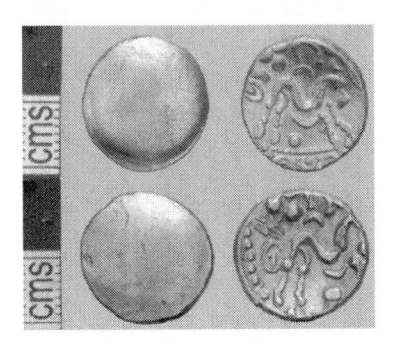

Gallic War Iron Age gold staters c. 50BC

And silver...

Aethelred the Unready silver penny, 978-1016

And copper-alloy...

Medieval seal matrix, a pelican in her piety, SUM PELICANUS DEI

And more gold...

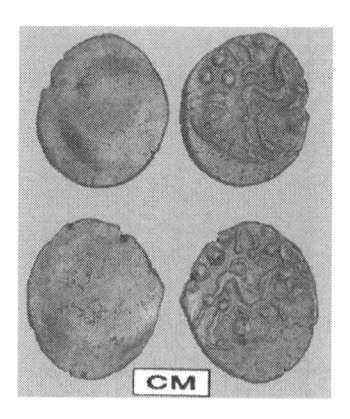

Gallic War Iron Age gold staters c. 50BC

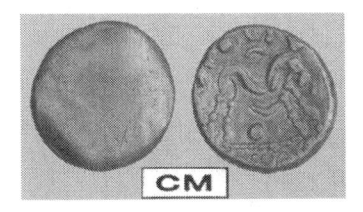

Gallic War Iron Age gold stater c. 50BC

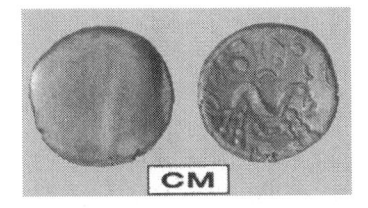

Gallic War Iron Age gold stater c. 50BC

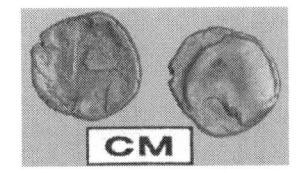

British Regini phallic geometric gold quarter stater c. 60-20BC

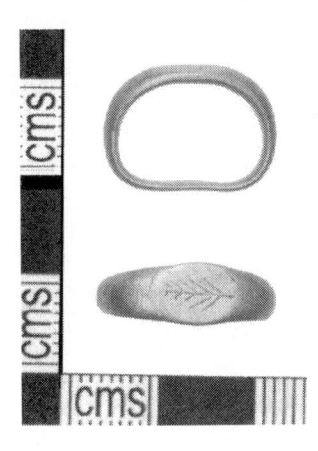

Roman gold finger ring with palm branch engraved on bezel, made in a D shape for wearing above the middle or top finger joint c. 3rd-4th centuries

Ancient gold is usually alloyed with silver but most modern gold coins are alloyed with copper. The Anderson or any copper-alloy dowsing rod baited with silver may still pick up modern gold coins because of their inherent attraction to copper. I have not yet found a modern gold coin with a baited rod but I only ever found one such coin as they are far from common on the sites I search. Nevertheless, it makes good sense on modern sites to alternate between using silver and gold bait to ensure finding modern gold coins and I recently started testing this approach. Switching to gold bait has, so far, not produced any solid gold objects but does produce gilded copper-alloy objects as well as copper-alloy coins and artifacts. Apart from low grade silver coins with 40-50% copper content, silver and lead almost disappeared from the range of finds. It may still be possible to find high silver content coins and artifacts using gold bait as they usually have a small copper content. Their absence may only be because I already found them using silver bait.

I should say that I still use the baited L-rod, particularly on the beach. The Anderson PMR-II is not submersible, so it is unwise to use it in wet places. Also the Anderson PMR-II does not sit comfortably on my beach detector as it does on my inland detector. It would cost almost nothing to replace my L-rod if it became necessary but replacing the Anderson PMR-II would be rather expensive.

In conclusion, there is clearly a little-recognised attractive force between like metals that can be tapped into, using the ancient art of dowsing. The best way to use this force for metal detecting is to use an L-rod in one hand to guide your detector in your other hand. Your finds rate and quality will greatly improve, for almost zero cost. A copper-alloy L-rod baited with gold or silver will further improve finds rate and quality. Start with home made rods and once you are happy all is working well, you may want to invest in a commercial L-rod. I thoroughly recommend the Anderson PMR-II.

14 METAL DETECTORS AND SEARCH HEADS

The basic requirements for metal detecting are a metal detector, a digging implement and somewhere to store your finds safely, while detecting. There are also a number of accessories that you might consider once you have started and decided you like the hobby – these are headphones, pinpoint probe, additional search head(s) and perhaps a hand held Global Positioning System. Stout and weatherproof clothing and footwear is also important plus depending on the temperature, sunscreen, insect repellent and a water bottle.

There is an overwhelming array of metal detectors to choose from. If you already own a metal detector, then you have probably made a good choice and frankly any metal detector worth its name will perform the task reasonably well. For those of you who do not already own a metal detector, I will make a few suggestions but the final choice of what to buy must be yours. I've lost count of the number of times I've heard the question: "Which metal detector is best?" The question should really be: "Which metal detector is best for me?" For the answer depends very much on you and your requirements. How fit are you? Do you want to search beaches, rivers, farmland, underwater?

One thing to consider very carefully is the weight and balance of the detector – you can get an aching arm very quickly swinging a heavy or badly balanced detector. Hip or chest mounting the control box is an option for many detectors and it will take the weight off your arm but the box may then get in the way when you dig. You can also buy a bungee harness to effectively reduce the weight of your detector. I would always advise seeing and handling the metal detector before you decide to buy, which is probably best achieved by visiting one of the many specialist dealers.

The vast majority of metal detectors are designed for finding coins, jewelry and similar sized artifacts in the top few inches of ground on inland sites while discriminating out the undesirable contaminants: iron and aluminum foil, for that is what most participants of the metal detecting hobby want. Iron is a major contaminant on farmland and aluminum foil abounds on dry beaches and recreational areas. Most popular machines work on a Very Low Frequency, Transmit/Receive system, discriminate audibly and/or visually and use the motion system of ground canceling. Ground canceling nulls effects from minerals in the ground and the motion system requires the machine to be kept moving; otherwise desirable objects are also canceled out. The system actually works a lot better than might be imagined. To pinpoint a target there is usually a selectable non-motion all metal mode, although it is easy enough to pinpoint in motion mode by passing the head over the target in a cross pattern. Machines at the lower end of the market may be non-motion and may have little or no discrimination although by nature, these types are fairly insensitive to iron but very sensitive to aluminum foil.

Within the motion detector range there are choices to be made regarding the desired amount of user control over the machine's electronic operation. Manufacturers are clearly split between simple 'switch on and go' and fully programmable detectors; some manufacturer's making only one type and some making both types. Logically the computer controlled programmable type will be better able to maximize depth and sort out the trash from the cash but you could spend a great deal of time messing about with the settings trying to achieve perfection instead of getting on with the searching. My own view is that if you are getting at all involved with dowsing then that will more than make up for any advantages of the computer control without the complexities but at the end of the day the choice between simplicity or bells and whistles is entirely yours. Whites has been the traditional UK choice for programmable types but C-Scope, Garrett, Minelab, XP and others also offer programmable models, with Minelab and XP leading.

A less popular type of hobby metal detector works on a principle known as pulse induction which is a non-motion (the detector signals a target whether moving or stationary) deep seeking system. These machines are notoriously sensitive to iron and very few discriminate between ferrous and non-ferrous metals (those that do discriminate tend to reject some desirable objects.) Pulse machines are firm favorites among beachcombers and underwater treasure hunters because of their ability to reach greater depths on most targets, typically twice that of many VLF machines and to cut through severe mineralization such as black sand.

There are two types of very specialized machines generally available, one being underwater detectors which are sealed to keep out water and constructed to withstand the pressures encountered in deep water. The other specialty is the so-called hoard or cache hunters, which are usually some sort of 'two-box' design, carried like a suitcase, rather than a forearm extension as with conventional detectors. Hoard hunters are designed to find only large objects, the size of a pint (565ml) pot upwards. They do not discriminate between ferrous and non-ferrous metals as treasure may be buried in an iron container (detectors cannot usually detect through metal) and they are very deep seeking, capable of probing several feet into the ground.

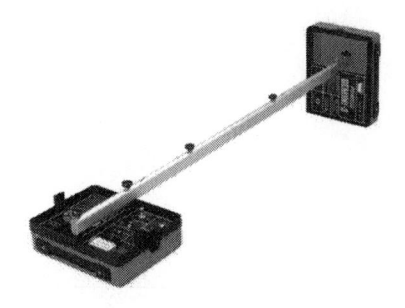

Fisher Gemini 3 hoard hunter

The choice of machine is very much dependent on what you want to do with it. Bear in mind that as the price of detectors rise you are generally paying for more features and the increase in performance over the cheaper machine can be quite marginal. I would advise a complete novice to go for a basic machine and, all things being equal, going for one of the lower priced ones from their own Country. They are better value for money and probably more suitable for the conditions. Typically if you buy an American machine in Britain you pay pound on the dollar and the conditions and even the artifacts which are looked for are quite different in the two Countries. Consider also that if you decide not to continue with the hobby your new machine will lose around 25% of its value if you have to sell. Amongst the higher priced detectors, foreign technology may be superior to your Country's and there may be less advantage in going for the home produced model. Foreign detectors made for the British market have a large following: Laser, Minelab and Whites particularly.

With the benefit of hindsight, if I was a serious beginner in Europe, I would buy a Laser B1 or one of its successors, the Rapier or Hawkeye. To keep the cost down, I could buy used or spread the cost on interest-free credit. An alternative is to contact a local dealer and see what he recommends for you but do not be persuaded to spend a large amount of money on a bright shiny all-singing, all-dancing detector that you may well find you cannot get on with. You can always upgrade from a basic model later, when you have some experience. I am also going to stick my neck out and suggest three starter machines to consider, which I haven't personally used but they all have a good reputation: C-Scope CS1MX, Fisher F2 or Garrett Ace 150 (or 250) these are all recommended for inland sites and dry beaches only but the Garrett is also said to perform reasonably well on salt wet beaches (I haven't tried it, so check this out yourself if wet beach searching is important).

CURRENT POPULAR METAL DETECTORS

MAKE	ORIGIN	TYPE
BOUNTY HUNTER	USA	VLF
C-SCOPE	UK	VLF
C-SCOPE	UK	PULSE INDUCTION
FISHER	USA	VLF
GARRETT	USA	VLF
LASER (TESORO)	USA FOR UK MARKET	VLF
MINELAB	AUSTRALIA/EIRE	VLF
TESORO	USA	VLF
VIKING	UK	VLF
WHITE'S	USA/UK	VLF
WHITE'S	USA/UK	PULSE INDUCTION
XP	FRANCE	VLF

Laser B1 metal detector

As a general rule the more expensive the metal detector the greater the depth to which it will be able to detect buried objects but it certainly isn't twice the price equals twice the depth and depth is not everything, especially on trashy sites. If you expect to search mainly inland then a VLF machine will be most suitable. If you want to search only beaches then a pulse machine may be more suitable but bearing in mind the lack of discrimination on Pulse Induction machines, it may be preferable to go for a VLF machine with a good reputation on beaches such as Whites or Minelab.

Anyone who spends a lot of time detecting usually has more than one metal detector. I personally have five – A Detech EDS as my main machine, a

Laser B1 Hi-Power as back-up and for heavily contaminated sites, a Minelab Sovereign XS2aPro, which I use mainly for beaches along with a C-Scope CS4PI and a Detech SSP-3000 pulse induction for beaches and deep seeking work. I also have a selection of search heads for all machines except the C-Scope. I wouldn't suggest that my selection represents the absolute best in metal detecting technology but, in conjunction with dowsing, it does allow me to perform well over a wide variety of sites and conditions.

Search heads (coils)

The search head contains one or more electrical coils and while the terms head and coil are used interchangeably, here I will refer to the head as the whole unit and the coil as the internal electrical wiring. The standard search head size fitted to the majority of detectors is around eight inches (20cm) diameter, which is a compromise to enable the detector to perform reasonably well under a variety of conditions. Most manufacturers produce a range of optional search head sizes typically from 3.5 inches (9cm) up to 15 inches (38cm) diameter and these can be employed to improve performance under certain conditions. As a rule of thumb the larger the search head the deeper it will detect but they have their disadvantages too: less sensitivity to smaller targets, more difficult to use on heavily mineralized or iron contaminated ground and less accurate pinpointing. Larger search heads are also heavier and more cumbersome to use although the weight can be compensated for by hip or chest mounting the detector control box, if the machine has that facility, or by using a bungee harness.

In addition to search head size variation, there are three different types of coil construction: concentric, 2D or wide scan and symmetrical electromagnetic field or SEF. Concentric coils, usually fitted to metal detectors as standard, have an inverted cone detection pattern, which achieves maximum depth only at the center of the search head. Wide scan coils have a pudding basin shaped detection pattern and while they don't achieve as great a depth as the same size concentric coil they do take in a larger volume of ground per sweep. If fast ground coverage is your prime concern, the wide scan coil is better and if you need greater depth the concentric coil is better. Now you can have the best of both worlds as the newly introduced symmetrical electromagnetic field or SEF coils combine both wide scan and concentric coils in one.

I strongly advise that you always fit a scuff cover or skid plate to protect the bottom of the search head from wearing through scraping the ground and obstructions. The scuff cover or search head protector is basically a plastic 'lid' that fits over the bottom of the search head and takes the wear and knocks. They do wear out but only cost about a tenth of the price of the search head itself to replace.

To find out where to buy metal detectors and accessories, the short answer is to look through a recent metal detecting magazine for your nearest supplier or Google it as they say.

15 PHOTOGRAPHING TREASURE AURAS

If you ever wondered how South American civilizations, like the Incas, found all their gold and silver, the answer is that at the height of the full moon, the Indians would see a bluish-green flame glowing above the ground where precious metal was buried. The Indians and later the Spanish Conquistadors used these auras to locate large quantities of silver and gold. If you are not too keen on wandering about in the middle of the night hoping to chance upon an aura, there is an alternative – the Polaroid SX-70 camera.

The Polaroid SX-70 camera, by accident rather than design, has the ability to 'see' auras emanating from buried precious metals. The quantity of buried metal doesn't have to be large for I have photographed auras emanating form single gold coins. The only criterion is that the metal needs to have been buried for at least a couple of years. A few years ago Polaroid ceased production and were bought out by enthusiasts who call themselves the Impossible Project https://shop.the-impossible-project.com/ They are making film but keep changing the name, it has been called PX-70 but now is called SX-70 film again, and it is the color version that we use. The camera itself is, uniquely amongst Polaroid field cameras, a Single Lens Reflex (which means viewing is accomplished directly through the lens instead of a parallel viewfinder or rangefinder). 'The only camera Polaroid ever made that was worth a damn,' some say.

Unfortunately, the SX-70, a success of the 1970s is no longer in production as such, although the Impossible Project is offering reconditioned models. Cameras can also be sought out on the second-hand market. I bought mine through a wanted advertisement in my local 'free ads' paper and I spotted two others recently: one on Ebay and a special edition SX-70, in the collectors section of a camera store. Other places you might look for a camera to buy are: boot fairs, antique stores, flea markets, second-hand stores, charity/thrift stores, yard/garage sales and photographic equipment fairs. Be aware there are SX-70 cameras and cameras using SX-70 film which are not SLR and it is the folding camera that is the real McCoy.

You will also need to get a UV filter to fit over the lens. There isn't a fitting on the lens to take a filter and as far as I know no filters were ever made for this camera, although there are clip on lenses which, if you get hold of one, could be adapted to take a filter. You won't go too far wrong if you take your camera to a camera store and ask them to supply a filter a little larger in diameter than the lens; 30mm diameter is about right but check that the filter will fit your camera before you leave the store. When you come to use the camera attach the filter with a couple of blobs of a solid reusable adhesive like 'Blu-Tack' or 'poster putty', one either side of the lens but not obscuring it. Don't stick the filter on with super-glue or you won't be able to close the camera up. Finally, one accessory that it would be useful to have is a magnetic compass; it doesn't need to be fancy as you only use it to identify North and South.

Having equipped yourself with SX-70 camera, film, UV filter and compass you only need a site where you think there could be gold or silver, which was buried more than two years ago. The optimum condition for taking pictures is either early morning sunlight or late evening sunlight. Foggy mornings are also said to produce good results. Presumably a low angle, of sunlight and possibly reduced light is needed for the camera to capture the aura. You may be successful outside of these conditions but if you don't know for sure where the treasure is you will give yourself the best chance if you follow the guidelines. You can always experiment later, when you have more experience.

Aim to be at your treasure site either at sunrise or a half-hour before sunset. Stand as close as you can to the area where you think (or your dowsing has suggested) precious metal may be buried and, using the compass, position yourself to the North or South of the target area so that you are at right angles to the sun. Focus the camera on the target area and take a photograph. As I am sure you know, Polaroid photographs are self processing and you will have your picture within a few minutes of clicking the shutter. Take a look at the photograph to see if it shows an aura. You may be lucky and get an aura first time or you may have to keep trying, perhaps shifting your position backwards or forwards or to the opposite side of the target area. Take a series of photographs over the half-hour period after sunrise or before sunset, as necessary. Persevere and you will soon find your aura and the treasure that produced it.

The Polaroid SX-70 photographs below were taken on sites believed to hold gold treasures. The auras were gold or yellow in color. On a site believed to hold a hoard of silver coins, not yet recovered, auras were produced which were purple in color. If the camera produces an aura, regardless of the color, I would suggest that you investigate the source.

Auras from a field which produced a scatter of gold coins

Aura from possible treasure wreck site

It has now become possible to capture auras using digital cameras and this is fully covered in my book, **The Successful Treasure Hunter's Secret Manual**. Please see chapter 21 for more details.

16 RESEARCH

No matter how good your dowsing, it is vital that you do some research for if you don't know what you are looking for with some degree of certainty then how can you hope to find it? You also need to identify the best potential sites as you might be spending hours on a field chasing a few old copper coins when you could be looking for a pot of gold coins on the next. It is true that dowsing allows you to be less precise with your research as you only need to identify what treasure you want to dowse for and its approximate location, for you can use your dowsing to home in with a fair degree of precision. The other great advantage of research is that you can use it to convince a landowner that there is something buried on his land and so hopefully gain search permission. In the absence of other evidence, very few people will accept a dowser's word that a treasure exists so if you have to convince someone to give you permission or to supply resources then it is almost essential that you have some research to show them.

Research can take many forms and you should become involved in at least some of them. You can if you wish use dowsing to decide which form research should take – simply ask your pendulum or L-rod whether a particular form of research is the best one to use in your own case. Check all the possibilities and go with the YES answers. You can even select a book from a shelf or list and a page in a book in the same way if you want. Is this book the best one to use? Will this book tell me what I'm looking for? Is the information I want on page 100? Is the information before page 100? Is it after page 100? Etc.

By research you are, as a generalization, trying to identify places where people in the past lived, worked, played and particularly where they might have lost valuables or buried their cash. Banks are a fairly recent innovation and many people never trusted banks anyway and still don't. As a dowser you have a great advantage over other treasure hunters because you can locate treasure from a distance. You only need a rough idea of where treasure might be; you do not need the precise details because you can lead yourself to the treasure. And don't forget to ask your rod or pendulum if the treasure has already been found or you could end up on a wild goose chase.

Main Research Sources

*Your local library

I have yet to find a public library that did not have a local history section and even if you find such a library they can obtain suitable material for you or direct you to an alternative library. The nearest library to your area of interest is the starting place for research. They will have books, pamphlets and maps covering the history of their local area, as well as being staffed by helpful people who can advise on your research. Consider also local history societies and museums although you will probably have to pay to use their libraries.

*Other people's research on potential treasure sites

In earlier years of treasure hunting there were numerous treasure site guides produced such as those by Thomas P Terry, of which some are still around, while newer ones, such as my own, UK, **Successful Detecting Sites**, have been published. You might think that the sites have been thoroughly gone over but in my experience hardly anyone bothers with them, probably because they think everyone else has already beaten them to it. You should also bear in mind that even if a treasure exists it may not have been found. My own Iron Age gold coin hoard eluded me for years and only started to turn up after the field was ploughed for the first time in a decade.

The only problem I found when I tried a selection of these sites was getting search permission, mainly because nearly all the sites I looked at were owned by commercial organizations. (There was an Abbey treasure on land owned by a builder and an Iron Age treasure on land owned by a mining company, for instance.) But don't let that put you off, you only need one land owner to say yes to a request for search permission.

*Local History Books

There are a vast number of Local History books around, any of which may have leads to interesting sites. I am particularly fond of the older or so-called antiquarian histories as they give eyewitness accounts of places as they were 100-200 years ago or more. An excellent place to start in the UK is The Victoria County History series, which began in the early years of the 20th century and covers most of England from prehistoric times to the Victorian era. The other county history series worth looking at are the Domesday Book translations inexpensively published by Phillimore, which give an eyewitness account of England more than 900 years ago. These are particularly useful for finding Saxon sites such as lost settlements, mills and other buildings which could lead to rare and valuable Saxon treasures. In addition to the Victoria History most areas have at least one antiquarian who travelled the highways and byways writing about what he saw; what he was told and what he researched. Your local library is bound to have something along these lines. Also look out for more modern printed material such as local travel guides, walking, hiking, rambling, cycling, camping and other outdoor books, which usually discuss local history to add interest.

*Landscape features

Rivers, streams, springs, wells, ponds etc., were vital from ancient times to fairly recently. They supplied water for survival and rivers often supplied an efficient means of transport and power for mills. Iron Age people worshipped water gods making offerings in and around water sites. The Romans were in the habit of throwing coins into rivers whenever they crossed them and they sometimes buried caches around the point where a Roman road crossed a river. The Saxons built watermills alongside rivers, which may have lasted well into medieval times. Trading would have taken place around these mills as the farmer had to pay the miller to grind his corn. Coins and other objects would have been lost, many of which could be very valuable today.

Old buildings such as castles, manors, mansions and churches. The church was the focal point of a community and there would have been fairs and other gatherings around old churches not to mention the possible hiding of the church's treasures.

Hedge boundaries might be evidence of earlier human activity. Plant species like blackthorn, holly and whych-hazel indicate centuries of human presence. Varying soil colors are evidence of previous habitation. Crop marks, produced because foundations reduce growth, while ditches increase growth, can indicate lost buildings and settlements.

*Places where caches have been previously found

Caches often turn up in multiples for at least a couple of reasons, one being that savings would be divided into two or three lots so that all wouldn't be lost if someone stumbled on their hiding place. Another reason is that an event such as an imminent attack triggered off a spate of cache burying by several people living in the same place, all at the same time.

*Local Knowledge

Never miss the opportunity of chatting to the older inhabitants of any place you may be interested in, they can often tell you snippets of information that will aid your searches. Also well worth tracking down is the, usually at least one, local historian who knows just about everything there is to know about a place. Don't forget farm workers either. They are usually very knowledgeable about matters relating to the land and will often surprise you with just what they do know. I'll never forget a casual laborer walking up to me while I was searching a site saying: "There was a Roman battle fought here, you know." According to one local historian he was absolutely right and I did find Roman coins there.

*Maps

Modern maps are essential for dowsing and subsequently finding the targets you have dowsed. In the UK the current popular Ordnance Survey maps are the Landranger at a scale of one and a quarter inches to one mile or 2cm to 1km and the old Pathfinder or new Explorer at double the scale i.e. two and a half inches to one mile or 4cm to 1km. The larger scale Pathfinder or Explorer is much better for our purposes as it contains more detail. You can gain much information by comparing old maps with modern maps such as the sites of lost buildings, track ways, changed river courses etc. Particularly useful for this purpose are the larger scale nineteenth or early twentieth century maps. Both old and newer maps will be available at public libraries serving the area covered by the map or main record offices for larger or other areas. Many metal detector retailers carry useful map series and old and current maps are available on line.

Another series of maps, in Britain which are excellent for research are the tithe maps produced for almost every rural parish in the Country following the Tithe Commutation Act of 1836. These are large scale maps, typically 12 inches to one mile or 20cm to one kilometer showing every building and field in the parish. Every field or plot of land is numbered and by referring the field number to an attached document called the apportionment we can find the name of the field, what its use was, its area, tenant and landowner. Particularly important for research is the name of the field from which we might, with care, gain some clues as to what went on there in the past. For instance a field called *Pennypot* probably gave up a cache of medieval pennies. I say 'with care' because *Penny Field* is more likely to refer to a rent payable of one penny. Your dowsing should sort the wheat from the chaff or consult a field name dictionary.

17 PUTTING IT ALL TOGETHER

There are many claims of treasure finds through the use of dowsing although they tend to be abroad rather than in the British Isles and some have to be taken with a pinch of salt. To show you how it has been done by others I'm going to relate four accounts which I know to be true and can be proven, the first two concern Jimmy Longton's finds, the second two, my own. The basic formula for dowsing for treasure is fairly simple:

*Find a potential treasure site by research, experience or accident

*Dowse a map, chart or photograph of the site to check if the treasure exists and to find its approximate location

*Locate the treasure using any means at your disposal

*Recover the treasure

The Penrith Hoard

In 1990 metal detectorist, Gerald Carter, discovered by researching local histories, that one hundred years or more earlier, two silver Viking brooches had been found in a field, not far from his home. The field was called Silver Field. Realizing that there might be more silver remaining in the ground, Gerald contacted Jimmy Longton and asked him to dowse a map of the field. Jimmy dowsed the map and announced that there was indeed more silver scattered over a circle, one hundred yards or meters in diameter. The two of them contacted the landowner and explained their findings. Permission to search the field was granted. Jimmy used his dowsing rod to pinpoint the hotspots, marking them with flags, while Gerald used his metal detector to check for metal. Their final haul, handed in to their local museum under the former treasure trove practice, consisted of six brooches - three intact and three in pieces. The British Museum retained the brooches and an award of £42,200 ($60,000) was shared between the finders and landowner.

The Secret Treasure of Charles I

Almost everyone knows that Charles I, the only British Monarch to be executed by his subjects, lost his head but very few know that he also lost a vast treasure, not once, but twice! The second treasure was melted down by Cromwell and largely consisted of an expensive replacement for the first, lost in Scotland's Firth of Forth in 1633.

In 1625 Charles I was crowned King of England but Scotland was a separate Kingdom and Charles also had to be crowned there. It was eight years before the King set off for his Scottish Coronation departing London on 10 May 1633 with an entourage of 150 English Lords, royal guards, servants and baggage. Travelling overland, the King arrived in Edinburgh nearly five weeks later to be crowned in the Abbey Church of Holyrood on Tuesday 18 June 1633.

It was customary for the Monarch to carry his personal finery with him so that he could entertain and be entertained in the manner to which he was accustomed. Amongst his baggage was a 230 piece silver gilt service from which a string of earlier monarchs had dined. As his Coronation tour began the King was showered with expensive gifts from his Scottish subjects, which grew as the days passed. The planned itinerary was to last well into July, visiting Linlithgow, Sterling, Dunfermline, Falkland and back to Edinburgh. At Falkland the King cut short his stay to make an unscheduled visit to Perth where he had arranged a highland gathering to entertain the party. But the King was growing tired and anxious to return to London.

On the morning of 9 July the King was back at Falkland Palace where his staff made ready for the journey home. At three o'clock the following morning, in deteriorating weather conditions, the King and major entourage with the most valuable baggage, left for Burntisland ferry to take the shortest route back to Edinburgh across the Firth of Forth. His Majesty's warship, the *Dreadnought*, having sailed from London as part of the supply train, anchored off the harbor waiting to transport the party in reasonable comfort across the water to Edinburgh's port of Leith. The King was transferred to the *Dreadnought* by pinnace but the ferry-boat following behind, *The Blessing of Burntisland*, heavily laden with baggage-wagons, was caught in a sudden squall, keeled over and sank. Of the 35 men on board the ferry, only two survived.

The loss of the Royal baggage and many friends was sad and embarrassing for Charles. He changed his plan of returning to London on the *Dreadnought* and travelled overland, either so all could see he was still alive and well or to avoid the sea, or both. Later, perhaps to avoid the Scottish clergy interpreting the loss as "an act of God", a group of Lancashire witches were executed for the sinking and the whole episode passed into obscurity.

In the 1980s, Robert (Bob) Brydon, a top historical researcher in Edinburgh, stumbled upon the story. Bob realized that, apart from the historical interest, he had probably found the key to the greatest treasure loss in Britain. Bob was keen to search for the lost ferry. Unfortunately all his contacts who could have assisted him were engaged in other projects.

The search was shelved until 1991 when Bob met up with Howard Murray a leading marine conservationist who had worked on the recovery of Henry VIII's ship, the *Mary Rose*. Howard was intrigued by the story and contacted his friend Martin Rhydderech, another historical researcher. They spent several weeks going over Bob's work and eventually found a new piece of information detailing all the silverware that had to be replaced following Charles' Scottish coronation – about half a ton (tonne)!

Now that they had definite proof that the treasure had been lost they only had to find it! But difficult conditions in the Firth of Forth meant it wasn't going to be easy. Poor underwater visibility and strong currents made searching for a wreck buried deep in the mud, an expensive and time consuming prospect needing more resources than Howard and Martin had.

Local entrepreneur Alec Kilgour then became involved. He managed to persuade the Forth Ports Authority to provide a survey vessel and British Gas to provide some revolutionary undersea oil exploration equipment. Bentech, a Norwegian Company also chipped in by lending a sonar system. All through the summer of 1992 the team scoured the Forth for wrecks. By the end of the summer they had identified over 200 targets in the two square mile search area which historical research had defined.

The next stage was to check each target out with divers but winter was beginning and they were almost out of funds. They attempted to find investors but investors wanted to sell any treasure recovered, which didn't fit in with the team's plan of conservation and display.

Alec then read of a similar project in the United States. Barry Clifford, a professional treasure hunter had discovered the *Whydah*, an 18th century pirate galleon buried in mud in only 30 feet of water. Alec contacted Barry and that summer (1993) the search really began. Barry and his team of American divers occasionally aided and abetted by Prince Andrew and the Royal Navy investigated many of the targets. But despite a diligent search lasting three years, they failed to find anything earlier then the 18th century and went home.

The search all but dried up during 1996 but in 1997 a friend of Alec Kilgour named Ian Archibald contacted the original team and the search recommenced. Apart from his diving and map skills, Ian knew dowser Jimmy Longton and although skeptical went to Lancashire to see him. Jimmy dowsed some charts with the pendulum and later travelled to Burntisland for a spot of 'field' dowsing. Ian took Jimmy out in a dive boat and navigated by pointing the boat in the direction indicated by Jimmy's dowsing rod. Suddenly, Jimmy's rod started swinging wildly, out of control. They stopped the boat and Ian was amazed to discover they were within a few meters of the spot Jimmy had marked on the chart; in fact Jimmy was more accurate than the global positioning system of the time. Jimmy was also amazed, as he had not experienced the rod's wild gyrations before. He now believes the rod followed the course of the *Blessing of Burntisland* as it ran into trouble all those years ago.

Several months later Ian was able to verify a wreck of the right dimensions and the right age right at the spot Jimmy indicated. Diving is extremely difficult; the tides only allowing 20 minutes access per day, the wreck is deep in the mud. A few shards of seventeenth century pottery have been brought up, some with the name Longton on it. Everyone involved believes they have found King Charles' treasure ship but it has yet to be confirmed.

The Roman Dump

Brian, a fellow member of my detecting club who has fallen in with the aristocracy, searches land, which adjoins my favorite farm. Consequently, we both take a keen interest in what each other is finding and where. A while back, Brian was asked to look for a pair of Jacobean pistols which were supposed to have been hidden somewhere in the landowner's house. At the club meeting following his search, Brian said to me: "I was over at her Ladyship's place the other day, looking for those pistols I told you about. You'll never guess what I found." "You found the pistols?" I replied. "No I didn't", sighed Brian, "But I found a cupboard full of Roman stuff with a letter from an archaeologist saying that it came from those fields you go on. You know, those her Ladyship used to own, years ago." "You're pulling my leg! I've spent hours and hours over there and all I've got to show for it is the finest collection of shotgun cartridge ends known to man." "Well, the archaeologist called it a Roman dump. It's there somewhere; you'll just have to find it."

'This is a job for Jimmy Longton', I thought and sent him a map of the farm. When the map came back, Jim had successfully identified areas where I had already found numerous coins and artifacts and had placed the Roman "dump" in a small copse. I tried to search the copse but it was too dense and I abandoned it without success. There was, however, a small field next to the copse which had defied being searched twice before, owing to one inch (2.5cm) thick kale stubble on the first occasion and frozen ground the second.

As luck would have it, I had no sooner given up on the copse when the farmer ploughed this small field. I started searching as close to the copse as I could get and was soon holding a Roman coin. By the time the field was drilled the total finds amounted to over forty Roman coins, a medieval ring and several other artifacts.

A few months later, after the field was ploughed again, I was rewarded with my first Iron Age gold stater coin as well as more Roman coins and a Roman brooch. Okay, I admit the finds aren't spectacular but without map dowsing they would almost certainly still be in the ground.

Silver Antoninianus of Valerian I, 253-260

Gold for the Gods

Although Jimmy Longton, Frank Delamere and I had dowsed maps of a particular farm, we all failed to identify the potential in one particular field. The problem, I think, was an abundance of targets at the other end of the farm which kept me busy digging for a couple of years and yielded handfuls of Roman coins as well as other interesting coins and artifacts from the last two thousand years. Jimmy believes that the problem was that we were so focused on Roman we only dowsed for Roman.

Research had shown a possible Roman road running through the farm but little else. The dowsing did show up one thing though and that was that the targets lay mainly along a riverbank, which skirted several of the fields. And that was where I found most of the metal objects. I concentrated on searching along the river bank whether map dowsing had shown targets or not and while the most productive area in terms of quantity had already been found by map dowsing, a few nice pieces came up from parts where map dowsing hadn't shown anything. Such was the case with one small field at the end of the farm, which had been pasture for many years. Under pasture identifiable finds dated no earlier than medieval but the plough soon changed that.

Much to my chagrin at the time, the day the field was ploughed and rolled the farmer walked across the field and plucked a single Iron Age gold coin from the ground. The condition was almost as minted which suggested there might be more especially considering that the field sloped gently down to a ditch that had once held an impressive ring of bright water - a classic contender for an Iron Age sacred site where offerings might be made to their gods. The farmer showed me where he had found the coin and I searched carefully around the find spot with a metal detector. Dowsing doesn't work well on freshly plowed fields because of remanence so I pretty well searched the whole field with the metal detector over the next few weeks until the growing crop forced me to stop. The only two finds worth mentioning amounted to an Elizabeth I sixpence and a Scottish four pence coin of David II, both about fifteen hundred years later than the Iron Age.

The crop had been harvested for more than a month and I hadn't set foot on the field until the farmer asked why I didn't go and have another look. 'The weeds are knee high' I thought: 'And what's more I've already searched every square inch.' The question sounded somewhat rhetorical however, so saying "What a good idea!" I made my way to the field. 'Good idea indeed!' I thought as I struggled through the undergrowth making my way to the far side of the field where the farmer had found his coin. I eventually reached the spot the richer for one piece of lead and a plain button. As I turned at the field boundary, I noticed a relatively clear piece of ground a few meters away and headed for that. Just as I reached the patch a crisp signal stopped me in my tracks. I took out a trowel full of earth to be greeted by a gleaming gold disc lying on top of the little black spoil heap. I knew it was an Iron Age coin before I had even picked it up and amazingly within the hour I was holding a second gold coin. It was quite some minutes before I had recovered from the shock enough to carry on detecting.

I returned the next day for another go but the success of the previous day was not to be repeated. I had, however, brought a Polaroid SX-70 camera with me. As sunset approached, I set the camera and stood in the centre of a mentally described circle that surrounded the find spots of the three gold coins. I took the first shot of the lower part of the field where I had found the two coins and then stood staring at the developing print as bright yellow streaks formed around the find spots. I turned around and took another shot of the upper part of the field where the first coin had been found and saw five separate streaks develop, fainter than the previous print but definite nevertheless. These pictures seemed to indicate that there was more gold waiting to be found. That night, I sent copies of the photos to Frank Delamere, my dowser friend in Dublin to see what he made of them.

The following day I was back on the field with an arsenal of deeper seeking devices: an 11 inch (27.5cm) search coil on my Laser, my pulse induction detector and my dowsing rod. I selected the pulse induction and set about the field, going over the find spots. I was quite surprised at the quantity of non-ferrous metal that emerged although a little disappointed that none was gold.

It was another week before I was able to return to the field. During the week, Frank returned my Polaroids annotated with crosses. Frank had dowsed the pictures and come up with some interesting results. In addition to accurately predicting the find spots of the three gold coins already found, Frank suggested a total of seven gold coins, two silver coins and a hoard of gold artifacts remained unrecovered.

I continued searching over the following few weeks but nothing significant turned up until finally the plow returned. As if mocking all my previous effort, half an hour after searching the freshly ploughed field I was holding gold coin number four. The next two sessions produced no precious metal and I was beginning to believe that the field only gave up its gold on the initial search after plowing or harvesting. Christmas was now upon us and I took some time out to study the dowsed Polaroids. The last coin I had found was just outside the shot and the predicted finds were scattered randomly over a quarter of an acre. Instead of concentrating around the areas immediately around the previous finds as I had been, I thought it would be worthwhile to investigate the predicted find spots one by one.

An hour into the search on Boxing Day I recovered coin number five. At the start of my next search, on the second day of the new Millennium, I was a little perturbed to hear crackling noises in my headphones as I switched my detector on but dismissed it as arcing from an electric fence. Dusk was approaching with almost nothing in my finds bag when a piece of brass scrap I had just passed the coil over, failed to produce a signal. I unplugged the headphones and checked the detector, which reassuringly gave a clear signal over the brass scrap. I continued detecting expecting to go home with nothing for my foolishness in not spotting the headphone problem earlier but the Gods were forgiving that day for the last signal pointed out a gleaming gold crescent; of coin number six just breaking the surface. Before I had to abandon the field to the crop yet again, I added one more coin to the score, making the total a magnificent seven.

Occasionally things happen which defy belief. The next time the field was ploughed the farmer walked across the field and plucked another gold coin from the ground. I visited the field a couple of days later and within half an hour I spotted that unmistakable glint in the bottom of the hole. I knew the score before I picked the find up – farmers: two, dowsers: seven…

18 TREASURE HUNTING BASICS

Professional treasure hunters, although very few in number, have been around for centuries. Generally they mounted extensive search and recovery operations costing large sums of money well beyond the reach of the common man or woman. The invention of the Aqua-lung by Jacques Yves Cousteau opened up the world of undersea exploration and wreck hunting to many, however locating and salvaging a potential treasure wreck, would still be very costly. It takes much silver to look for gold it used to be said.

The development of the hobby metal detector in the USA in the 1960s changed all that and spawned popular treasure hunting. The new breed of treasure hunters in the USA, tend to search for relatively modern coin and jewelry losses on beaches and other recreational areas with the minority searching ghost towns, battle sites and prospecting for native gold. The hobby quickly spread to Britain where it is more popularly and less brashly called Metal Detecting and initially followed the same pattern of searching recreational areas. It was soon discovered that the farmland of Britain is relatively rich in lost metalwork from the last 2000-3000 years and in view of the greater interest and potentially greater reward for effort expended, most detectorists have migrated to the fields on a more or less permanent basis.

While probably not practiced to such a great extent as in Britain and the USA, treasure hunting has spread to other parts of the world. In Australia gold nugget hunting is popular. Holland seems to be the only other keen participant in Europe although this may be as a result of constraints imposed by law in many countries. In Southern Ireland for instance it is not illegal to use a metal detector but it is illegal to use a detector to search for archaeological objects. And if you use a metal detector, you are presumed to be searching for archaeological objects! The only way round this is to convince the authorities that you are not searching for archaeological objects – whether a claim that you dowsed the site beforehand and found it to be free of archaeological objects would stand up in court, I don't know.

Fortunately in Britain although we do have the Treasure Act to contend with (of which more later) the situation is much better providing we follow a few simple rules set out below.

It's not my job to pontificate, however I do urge you to follow the code of practice, or any code for your own country, for you own sake and the sake of the hobby. There is nothing in the code that isn't either common courtesy or common sense and you could get yourself into serious trouble by ignoring it, not necessarily just from the law either.

Treasure Hunting is not a dangerous hobby if followed sensibly but venturing into unknown territory could be, as an acquaintance of mine will testify. While detecting in a park where he didn't have permission (many would argue that he didn't need permission but I think it's always best to ask) he unearthed two glass vials with brass tops. Unrecognized, they ended up in his car along with other finds until, on the way home, the action of rolling around dislodged some of the dirt and he noticed they were marked "War Department." He took them to the Police. The Police called the Bomb Squad who identified them as nitro-glycerin before safely detonating them. The resulting explosion was heard ten miles away! Had he sought permission he might have been forewarned of the possible dangers.

Code of Practice for Responsible Detecting in England and Wales

Being responsible means:

Before you go metal-detecting

1. Not trespassing; before you start detecting obtain permission to search from the landowner/occupier, regardless of the status, or perceived status, of the land. Remember that all land has an owner. To avoid subsequent disputes it is always advisable to get permission and agreement in writing first regarding the ownership of any finds subsequently discovered (see http://www.cla.org.uk / http://www.nfuonline.com).

2. Adhering to the laws concerning protected sites (e.g. those defined as Scheduled Monuments or Sites of Special Scientific Interest: you can obtain details of these from the landowner/occupier, Finds Liaison Officer, Historic Environment Record or at http://www.magic.gov.uk). Take extra care when detecting near protected sites: for example, it is not always clear where the boundaries lie on the ground.

3. You are strongly recommended to join a metal detecting club or association that encourages co-operation and responsive exchanges with other responsible heritage groups. Details of metal detecting organizations can be found at http://www.ncmd.co.uk / http://www.fid.newbury.net.

4. Familiarising yourself with and following current conservation advice on the handling, care and storage of archaeological objects (see http://www.finds.org.uk).

While you are metal-detecting

5. Wherever possible working on ground that has already been disturbed (such as ploughed land or that which has formerly been ploughed), and only within the depth of ploughing. If detecting takes place on undisturbed pasture, be careful to ensure that no damage is done to the archaeological value of the land, including earthworks.

6. Minimising any ground disturbance through the use of suitable tools and by reinstating any excavated material as neatly as possible. Endeavour not to damage stratified archaeological deposits.

7. Recording findspots as accurately as possible for all finds (i.e. to at least a one hundred metre square, using an Ordnance Survey map or hand-held

Global Positioning Systems (GPS) device) whilst in the field. Bag finds individually and record the National Grid Reference (NGR) on the bag. Findspot information should not be passed on to other parties without the agreement of the landowner/occupier (see also clause 9).

8. Respecting the Country Code (leave gates and property as you find them and do not damage crops, frighten animals, or disturb ground nesting birds, and dispose properly of litter: see http://www.countrysideaccess.gov.uk).

After you have been metal-detecting

9. Reporting any finds to the relevant landowner/occupier; and (with the agreement of the landowner/occupier) to the Portable Antiquities Scheme, so the information can pass into the local Historic Environment Record. Both the Country Land and Business Association (http://www.cla.org.uk) and the National Farmers Union (http://www.nfuonline.com) support the reporting of finds. Details of your local Finds liaison Officer can be found at http://www.finds.org.uk, email info@finds.org.uk or phone 020 7323 8611.

10. Abiding by the provisions of the Treasure Act and Treasure Act Code of Practice (http://www.finds.org.uk), wreck law (http://www.mcga.gov.uk) and export licensing (http://www.mta.gov.uk). If you need advice your local Finds Liaison Officer will be able to help you.

11. Seeking expert help if you discover something large below the ploughsoil, or a concentration of finds or unusual material, or wreck remains, and ensuring that the landowner/occupier's permission is obtained to do so. Your local Finds Liaison Officer may be able to help or will be able to advise of an appropriate person. Reporting the find does not change your rights of discovery, but will result in far more archaeological evidence being discovered.

12. Calling the Police, and notifying the landowner/occupier, if you find any traces of human remains.

13. Calling the Police or HM Coastguard, and notifying the landowner/occupier, if you find anything that may be a live explosive: do not use a metal-detector or mobile phone nearby as this might trigger an explosion. Do not attempt to move or interfere with any such explosives.

Treasure Law

Regrettably there is no international law on metal detecting finds and the laws differ from country to country and even from State to State in the USA. Given below are a number of legal definitions that could apply to metal detecting finds together with the popular court ruling on finds made under each category:

Lost property, which has been involuntarily parted from its owner, belongs to the owner or their heirs and if they cannot be traced, title goes to the finder. You are legally obliged to take reasonable steps to return lost property to its owner. In the case of loose change it is highly unlikely you will find an owner, so that is yours to keep. However if you find a piece of jewelry, for example, you could report it to the local police, if lost property is in their remit, or take suitable action to find the owner such as advertising in a local newspaper or on social media. In Britain, the police generally disclaim lost property after one month. Although recently, as the police do not have a statutory duty to deal with lost property, some forces are no longer accepting lost property so, as long as you have made reasonable attempts to trace the owner it is yours to keep unless it may be evidence of a crime, is dangerous, illegal (e.g. an offensive weapon) or contains personal data. Bear in mind that the owner retains all rights to the item, so if he or she turns up later then they can still demand return of the item or all proceeds if the item has been sold.

Mislaid property, where the owner puts the object down and forgets about it, reverts to the site owner, if not claimed by the owner.

Abandoned property, which is simply thrown away, goes to the finder.

Embedded property refers to buried artifacts or even natural minerals, which fall outside the definition of treasure trove. Court rulings for such finds will generally be the same as for treasure trove.

Archaeological objects or portable antiquities may cover excavated objects as recent as 50 years old in some countries and states, which have to be reported to museum authorities or similar. A reward is often paid but check local laws. Export licenses may be required (e.g. European Economic Community) before such objects can be removed from the country.

Treasure trove, defined as objects made substantially of gold, silver and their alloys (plus paper money) hidden or concealed for several decades, with the intention of recovery, where the owners or heirs cannot be traced. Treasure trove finds on private land normally go to the finder, providing the finder wasn't trespassing but in the UK, treasure is normally shared equally between landowner and finder. If the finder was trespassing then finds go to the landowner or site owner. Finds on government land go to the government unless there is a prior agreement in place.

Wreck, being an abandoned vessel, or something abandoned off a vessel, which is afloat, stranded, aground or sunken. The salvager is normally entitled to a reward related to the value of the find.

By necessity the above is a simplification and before you spend a lot of time and money on the hunt, you would be wise to ascertain local law on finds. It would also be prudent to have a written agreement, with the landowner or site owner, on the distribution of finds (usually a 50/50 split between finder and landowner).

The Treasure Act in Britain

At present, treasure is defined, under the Act, as any object other than a coin, at least 300 years old when found, which has a metallic content, of which at least 10% by weight is gold or silver. And all coins that contain at least 10% by weight of gold or silver that come from the same find consisting of at least two coins, at least 300 years old. And all coins that contain less than 10% by weight gold or silver that come from the same find consisting of at least ten coins at least 300 years old. And any associated objects, except un-worked natural objects (e.g. a pot or other container), found in the same place as treasure objects. And any objects or coin hoards less than 300 years old, made substantially of gold and silver that have been deliberately hidden with the intention of recovery and for which the owner is unknown. Since 1 January 2003 the definition of treasure has been extended on prehistoric (i.e. up to the end of the Iron Age) finds to include all multiple artifacts, made of any metal, found together and single artifacts deliberately containing any quantity of precious metal.

The Act applies to objects found anywhere in England, Wales and Northern Ireland, including in or on land, in buildings (whether occupied or ruined), in rivers and lakes and on the foreshore (the area between mean high water and mean low water) providing the object does not come from a wreck. If the object has come from a wreck then it will be subject to the salvage regime that applies to wreck under the Merchant Shipping Act 1995. The Receiver of Wreck (located via Customs & Excise) must legally be notified of all property recovered following the loss of a vessel; and the salvager is entitled to a reward related to the value of the object, either from the owner, if identified, or the Crown.

If you are searching in other parts of the British Isles or outside of Britain altogether, you should familiarize yourself with treasure law for your specific area. In Scotland, for instance, all ownerless objects belong to the Crown. They must be reported regardless of where they were found or of what they are made. The finder receives market value as long as no laws have been broken. Not all finds will be claimed. Further information from: Treasure Trove Unit, National Museum of Scotland, Chambers Street, Edinburgh, EH1 1JF.

I have the experience of having had to report over a dozen separate finds of treasure since the introduction of the Treasure Act. While there were concerns over lack of confidentiality regarding the find spot in the early days, everything has settled down, generally working well and fairly to all parties involved. I still urge you to be cautious when reporting your finds, so here are my unofficial suggestions for protecting yourself and your landowner friends when you find potential treasure:

* Leave your treasure 'as found' and resist all temptation to clean or restore your find except for the absolute minimum necessary to identify it as possible treasure.

* The National Council for Metal Detecting will willingly advise in the process of reporting treasure and it is well worth involving them from the start when you have possible treasure to report.

* County Finds Liaison Officers (FLOs) are now heavily involved in the treasure process and will also advise and help.

* Your only legal obligation is to report the finding of potential treasure to the Coroner within fourteen days of becoming aware that it is possibly treasure.

* Discuss the matter with the landowner as soon as possible.

* Do the reporting yourself. The legal responsibility for reporting rests with

the finder and no one will look after your interests as well as you.

* Bear in mind, especially if you want to keep the coin, that the first coin found of a scattered hoard may not be treasure, if it was the only coin found on that occasion and there was sufficient time to sell the coin before the finding of the second coin.

* Report your find to the Coroner in writing within 14 days and keep a copy of the letter. In the first instance only report the find spot as the name of the parish in which the find was made. If it is not clear which Coroner needs to be informed, ask your FLO or write to the most likely Coroner and ask for your letter to be passed on, as necessary. In my area it is current practice for finds to be reported to the FLO in lieu of the Coroner. As this is not strictly the letter of the law, I report to the Coroner in writing and send a copy to the FLO.

* Always take photographs or have photographs taken of all possible views of all objects, before you hand the objects over. You will at least have something to show an independent valuation expert and, if you want to publish, there won't be any copyright or access issues.

* There is no time limit for handing over the find and you should be allowed a reasonable amount of time for such things as photographing, valuing, showing it to the landowner, displaying it at a club meeting etc. Bear in mind, however, that you are responsible for the security of the find until you hand it over.

* These days Finds Liaison Officers often collect potential treasure from finders, however you may be asked to deposit your find at a museum or FLO at your own expense. You are not legal obliged to take your find anywhere, however, if you can arrange this it is best to comply. Insist on being given the Treasure Receipt, (filled out in your presence) in exchange for your find.

* The Treasure Act Code of Practice requires that the precise find spot must be established and should be kept confidential. You can <u>insist</u> on the confidentiality requirement when the Treasure Receipt is completed and have the precise find spot kept separately.

* A section of the Treasure Receipt is labeled "Location of find spot". Only enter vague details of the find spot such as name of Parish, four-figure map reference or a nondescript name for the site such as 'Field A'.

* If a museum is interested in acquiring the find, a Coroner's Inquest will be arranged. You should be invited to attend the Inquest for which you can claim expenses and I suggest you should attend if you possibly can – you will at least know who was there and what was said. The press may be there, so be careful not to reveal find spot information if they are.

* Following an Inquest the Press will probably want to speak to you. Whether you speak to them is up to you but you can at least appeal for some confidentiality and perhaps avoid them uncovering, or inventing, more than you would like revealed.

* The final stumbling block is the valuation, which will be given via the Department for Culture Media and Sport some weeks after the Inquest. You need to know if the valuation is 'A Fair Market Value' so that you can decide whether to accept it. Fair market value is an attempt to arrive at the price you should expect to get if selling your find on the open market and the Treasure Valuation Committee tries to arrive at the 'hammer' price without auctioneer's deductions. Pick out a couple of dealers specializing in coins or objects similar to yours from the advertisements in treasure hunting magazines. Ask the dealers to give you their buying-in price for your find (send photographs if necessary). I am sure they will oblige for little or no charge. If the treasure is very rare it should be possible to arrange viewing for independent appraisal. You should be offered two opportunities to contest the valuation, one before the valuation committee meets and one after. I would accept the valuation if it falls within or above your dealers' ballpark figures and contest it if it falls below. If you are going to contest the valuation, get in before the committee meets if you can. There is a slight possibility that the museum involved may contest the valuation and succeed in getting it reduced – if this happens, unless there is clear justification, you could appeal against it all the way to the Secretary of State, if necessary.

* An alternative is for you or the landowner or both to refuse any award for the find when you first report it or at any time, preferably prior to any inquest. The find will then be offered to interested museums at a discount or free, if all parties refuse the award.

19 SEARCH AGREEMENTS

As money will probably be involved at some time during your searches, and disputes often arise over money, I advise you to try and get a signed, written search agreement at the outset. I have to say that landowners tend not to want to get involved with such things and I have only occasionally succeeded in getting one drawn up myself. However, I almost always request search permission in writing, including an offer to share the proceeds equally and I keep a copy of the letter. I don't pretend to be a lawyer but I am fairly sure that, if you do the same, then in the event of a dispute, the copy of your letter you have kept together with any written permission from the landowner would stand up as evidence of an agreement. I am sure I don't need to tell you to play fair with landowners, for their goodwill is essential to your pursuit of treasure.

In case you can get a landowner to sign an agreement, on the following page there is an example you may copy and use:

DAVID VILLANUEVA

LANDOWNER/SEARCHER AGREEMENT

The following terms and conditions are agreed between landowner and searcher:

The landowner grants permission to the searcher to use location equipment and hand tools to search and extract finds from the ground of land known as:
....
....

During the period: **From:**............................... **To:**..

The searcher enters the land at the searcher's own risk.

The searcher shall report all worthwhile finds to the landowner within a reasonable time of being found in accordance with the landowner's wishes.

The searcher shall report any bombs, missiles or live ammunition discovered, to the landowner and to the police.

Archaeological discoveries will be reported to the landowner in the first instance. The information will then be passed on to the local museum or archaeological body providing the landowner agrees.

Potential treasure discoveries will be reported to the landowner in the first instance providing this can be achieved within fourteen days. In any event the Coroner will be informed within fourteen days as prescribed by The Treasure Act.

All finds (or the value thereof) and treasure awards will be shared equally between the searcher and landowner.

The searcher shall take great care to: work tidily, avoid hindrance to the working of the land and avoid damage to the landowner's, property, animals or crops. In the unlikely event of damage the searcher shall rectify the damage at the searcher's own expense.

The searcher shall comply with any special conditions, recorded overleaf.

This agreement may be terminated by the landowner at any time and if so terminated the searcher shall immediately cease all operations.

	SEARCHER	**LANDOWNER**
SIGNATURE:	....	....
NAME:	....	....
ADDRESS:	....	....
	....	....
	....	....
DATE:	....	....

20 BIBLIOGRAPHY

Beasse, Pierre, **A New and Rational Treatise of Dowsing according to the methods of Physical Radiesthesie; Excluding any kind of occultism and open to everybody**, (Progres Scientifique, 1941, Mokelumne Hill, California, 1975)

Bird, Christopher, **Divining**, (London, 1980)

Cox, Bill, **The Psychology of Treasure Dowsing**, (Santa Barbara, California, 1989)

Davies, Rodney, **Dowsing**, (Aquarian Press, London, 1991)

Department for Culture, Media and Sport, **The Treasure Act 1996, Code of Practice (Revised), (England and Wales)**, (London SW1Y 5DH, 2002)

Fairley, John & Welfare, Simon, 'Water, Water, Everywhere', in **Arthur C Clarke's World of Strange Powers**, (London, 1984)

France, Henry De, **The Modern Dowser: A Guide to the Use of the Divining Rod and Pendulum**, (London, 1936); **The Elements of Dowsing** (London, 1951)

Graves, Tom, **Discover Dowsing**, (Aquarian Press, London, 1989); **The Dowser's Workbook**, (Aquarian Press, London, 1989)

Graves, Tom, & Hoult, Janet, Eds, **The Essential T. C. Lethbridge**, (London, 1980)

Lethbridge, T C, **The Power of the Pendulum**, (London, 1976, 1983)

Matacia, Louis J., **Finding Treasure Auras by Combining Science and Parapsychology**, (Bluemont, Virginia, 1996); **Finding Treasure Combining Science and Parapsychology**, (Bluemont, Virginia, 1997)

Maury, Marguerite, **How to Dowse: Experimental and Practical Radiesthesia**, (London, 1953)

Naylor, P, **Discover Dowsing and Divining**, (Shire Publications, 1991)

Nielsen, Greg & Polansky, Joseph, **Pendulum Power**, (Aquarian Press, London, 1986)

Scott Elliot, J, **Dowsing: One Man's Way**, (British Society of Dowsers, 1996)

Simmons, Russ, **Dowsing for Treasure**, (Dowsing Institute of America, 1984, 1988)

Stine, G Harry, **Amazing and Wonderful Mind Machines You Can Build**, (Largo, Florida, 1997)

Trinder, W H, **Dowsing**, (The British Society of Dowsers, 1939, 1941, 1948)

Welton, Thomas, **Jacob's Rod**, (London, 1874)

Wheatley, Dennis, **Principles of Dowsing**, (Thorsons, 2000)

21 BOOKS IN PRINT FROM THE SAME AUTHOR

THE SUCCESSFUL TREASURE HUNTER'S SECRET MANUAL: Discovering Treasure Auras in the Digital Age Soft Cover, 210mm x 146mm, (8.25 x 5.75 inches) 68 pages, (True Treasure Books, 2009) ISBN 978 0 9550325 5 4

(Also an E-Book under the title: THE SUCCESSFUL TREASURE HUNTER'S SECRET MANUAL: How to Use Modern Cameras to Locate Buried Metals, Gold, Silver, Coins, Caches...)

CLEANING COINS & ARTEFACTS: Conservation * Restoration * Presentation, Soft Cover, 210mm x 146mm, (8.25 x 5.75 inches) 110 pages, (Greenlight Publishing, 2008) ISBN 978 1 897738 337

(Also an E-Book under the title: THE SUCCESSFUL TREASURE HUNTER'S ESSENTIAL COIN AND RELIC MANAGER: How to Clean, Conserve, Display, Photograph, Repair, Restore, Replicate and Store Metal Detecting Finds)

PERMISSION IMPOSSIBLE: Metal Detecting Search Permission Made Easy, Soft Cover, 210mm x 146mm, (8.25 x 5.75 inches) 52 pages, (True Treasure Books, 2007) ISBN 978 0 9550325 3 0 (Also an E-Book)

SITE RESEARCH FOR DETECTORISTS, FIELDWALKERS & ARCHAEOLOGISTS, Soft Cover, 250mm x 190mm, (9.75 x 7.5 inches) 160 pages, (Greenlight Publishing, 2006) ISBN 1 897738 285

SUCCESSFUL DETECTING SITES: Locate 1000s of Superb Sites and Make More Finds, Soft Cover, 250mm x 190mm, (9.75 x 7.5 inches) 238 pages, (Greenlight Publishing, 2007) ISBN 978 1 897738 306

THE SUCCESSFUL TREASURE HUNTER'S ESSENTIAL SITE RESEARCH MANUAL: How to Find Productive Metal Detecting Sites, (E-Book)

THE ESSENTIAL GUIDE TO OLD, ANTIQUE AND ANCIENT METAL SPOONS, Soft Cover, 210mm x 146mm, 88 pages, (True Treasure Books, 2008) ISBN 978 0 9550325 4 7 (Also an E-Book)

THE SUCCESSFUL TREASURE HUNTER'S ESSENTIAL DOWSING MANUAL: How to Easily Develop Your Latent Skills to Find Treasure in Abundance, Soft Cover, 210mm x 146mm, (8.25 x 5.75 inches) 60 pages, (True Treasure Books, 2005) ISBN 0 9550325 0 4

(Also an E-Book under the title: THE SUCCESSFUL TREASURE HUNTER'S ESSENTIAL DOWSING MANUAL: How to Easily Develop Your Latent Skills to Locate Gold, Silver, Coins, Caches...)

MY ANCESTOR LEFT AN HEIRLOOM: Discovering Heirlooms and Ancestors Through the Metalwork They Left Behind, Soft Cover, 210mm x 146mm, (8.25 x 5.75 inches) 84 pages, (True Treasure Books, 2011) ISBN 978 0 9550325 6 1

(Also an E-Book under the title: MY ANCESTOR LEFT AN HEIRLOOM: Hunting Family History and Genealogy Treasure Through Metal Detecting Finds)

METAL DETECTING MADE EASY: A Guide for Beginners and Reference for All, Soft Cover, 210mm x 146mm, (8.25 x 5.75 inches) 128 pages, (True Treasure Books, 2014) ISBN 978 0 9550325 7 8 (Also an E-Book)

FAITHFUL ATTRACTION: How to Drive Your Metal Detector to Find Treasure (E-Book)

TOKENS & TRADERS OF KENT in the Seventeenth, Eighteenth & Nineteenth Centuries, Soft Cover, 215mm x 140mm, (8.5 x 5.5 inches) 112 pages, (True Treasure Books, 2015) ISBN 978 0 9550325 8 5 (Also an E-Book)

All books are available from True Treasure Books online at http://www.truetreasurebooks.net Also at Amazon, Kindle, Ebay.co.uk, Alibris, Smashwords.com, most UK bookstores and metal detector stores.

ABOUT THE AUTHOR

David Villanueva was born in Birmingham, England in 1951 where he grew up. In 1972 his mother bought him Ted Fletcher's book, **A Fortune Under Your Feet**, which inspired him to buy a BFO metal detector. The performance was very poor by current standards but it did find coins and David became hooked.

In 1985, a move to Kent, England saw David searching beaches with an old Pulse Induction detector. The machine's sensitivity to iron and zero discrimination did not suit local conditions, so he bought a new Induction Balance detector, which worked well on the dry beaches and encouraged him to try inland sites. He joined a metal detecting club and gained permission to search a small farm, making all manner of old and interesting finds. Having a keen interest in history, David researched his locality, which led to more productive sites to search and write about in a dozen books and the two British metal detecting magazines – **Treasure Hunting** and **The Searcher** – which have published more than two dozens of David's articles.

But it was a chance encounter with Britain's best treasure dowser, Jimmy Longton that supercharged David's treasure hunting. Jimmy, who had dowsed his way to a $60,000 Viking silver hoard, taught David how to dowse for treasure with remarkable results. David suddenly found himself reporting real treasures in the form of caches of ancient tools and gold coins as well as Roman, Saxon and medieval gold and silver jewelry. David has recorded over a dozen finds under the Treasure Act and maintains a shelf full of trophies won at the Swale Search and Recovery Club.

###

Printed in Great Britain
by Amazon